The 7 HABITS *of* Highly inEffective Churches

Why your church stopped growing and what to do about it

RON GLADDEN

Copyright © 2003 Ron Gladden

The author assumes full responsibility for the accuracy of all facts and quotations as cited in this book.

No part of this publication may be reproduced, stored in a retrieval system, or transmitted, in any form or by any means electronic, photocopied, recorded, or otherwise, without the prior written permission of the copyright holder.

Author: Ron Gladden
Technical edit: Sherri Cash
Cover design: Palimore Studios
Layout design: Ginger Calkins
Layout: Christal Gregerson

Additional copies of this book and *The 7 Habits of Highly Ineffective Churches* seminar on DVD or video are available from:
Advent*Source*
5040 Prescott Avenue
Lincoln, NE 68506
800-328-0525
www.adventsource.org

For more information on church planting or to schedule a live seminar at your church or conference contact:

Adventist Church Planting Center
P.O. Box 871150
Vancouver, WA 98687
(360) 816-1478
www.plantthefuture.org

Printed in the United States of America

ISBN# 1-57756-120-1

TABLE OF CONTENTS

Dave & Teresa Livermore • Dennis & Debbie Punford • Keith & Ann Trumbo • Daniel & Marilyn Suarez • Jody & Sonja Dickhaut • Boyd & Joella Lundell • Jay & Kendra Perry • Matt & Susan Segebartt • Steven & Gayla Shomler • Roger & Gail Walter • Gary & Jen Walter • Fran Gladden • Bruce & Laura Avery • Clarissa Worley • Doug & Dawn Venn • Brant & Shellie Berglin • Shane & Darlene Anderson • Steve & Melissa Leddy • Matthew & Susan Gamble • Cleveland Hobdy • Dennis & Anita McKown • Wayne & Jeanine Kablanow • Peter & Saundra Trzinski • Greg & Cheryl Griffitts • Brian & Michelle Yeager • Lavelle Whitehouse • Richie & Timi Brower • Geoff & Alicia Patterson • Don & Ruthie Jacobsen • Kurt & Janie Johnson • Phil & Debbie Muthersbaugh • David & Susan Woods • Dan Serns • Bill & Sally Miller • Robert & Peggy Wagley • David & Cindy Vandevere • Jim Brauer • Gordon Pifher • Jim & Linda Kincaid • John Freedman • Doug Bing • Jere & Nancy Wallack • Doug & Carole Kilcher • Ramon & Aurora Canals • Jim Gaull • Jonathan Penner • Dean & Gayle Coridan • Ed & Lillian Keyes • Kevin & Patricia Kuehmichel • Jim Snell • Lonnie Gienger • Michael & Luda Melnik • Tom Lemon • Freddie Russell • Jim Kilmer • Dave & Teresa Livermore • Dennis & Debbie Pumford • Keith
Lundell
Gail Wa
Doug & Dawn Venn • Brant & Shellie Berglin • Shane & Darlene Anderson • Steve & Melissa Leddy • Matthew & Susan ... Anita McKown • Wayne & Jeanine Kablanow • Peter & Saundra Trzinski • Greg & Cheryl Griffitts • Brian & Michelle Yeager • Lavelle Whitehouse ... Patterson • Don & Ruthie Jacobsen • Kurt & Janie Johnson • Phil & Debbie Muthersbaugh • David & Susan Woods • Dan Serns • Bill & Sally Miller ... Vandevere • Jim Brauer • Gordon Pifher • Jim & Linda Kincaid • John Freedman • Doug Bing • Jere & Nancy Wallack • Doug & Carole Kilcher • Ramon & Aurora Canals • Jim Gaull • Jonathan Penner • Dean & Gayle Coridan • Ed & ... Snell • Lonnie Gienger • Michael & Luda Melnik • Tom Lemon • Freddie Russell • Jim Kilmer • Dave & Teresa Livermore • Dennis & Debbie ... Daniel & Marilyn Suarez • Jody & Sonja Dickhaut • Boyd & Joella Lundell • Jay & Kendra Perry • Matt & Susan Segebartt • Steven & Gayla Shomler ... Walter • Fran Gladden • Bruce & Laura Avery • Clarissa Worley ... & Shellie Berglin • Shane & Darlene Anderson • Steve & Melissa Leddy • Matthew & Susan Gamble • Cleveland Hobdy • Dennis & Anita McKown • Wayne ... Saundra Trzinski • Greg & Cheryl Griffitts • Brian & Michelle Yeager • Lavelle Whitehouse • Richie & Timi Brower • Geoff & Alicia Patterson • Don & Ruthie Jacobsen • Kurt & Janie Johnson • Phil & Debbie Muthersbaugh • David & Susan Woods • Dan Serns • Bill & Sally Miller • Robert & Peggy Wagley • David & Cindy Vandevere • Jim Brauer • Gordon Pifher • Jim & Linda Kincaid • John Freedman • Doug Bing • Jere & Nancy Wallack • Doug & Carole Kilcher • Ramon & Aurora Canals • Jim Gaull • Jonathan Penner • Dean & Gayle Coridan • Ed & Lillian Keyes • Kevin & Patricia Kuehmichel • Jim Snell • Lonnie Gienger • Michael & Luda Melnik • Tom Lemon • Freddie Russell • Jim Kilmer • Dave & Teresa Livermore • Dennis & Debbie Pumford • Keith & Ann Trumbo • Daniel & Marilyn Suarez • Jody & Sonja Dickhaut • Boyd & Joella Lundell • Jay & Kendra Perry • Matt & Susan Segebartt • Steven & Gayla Shomler • Roger & Gail Walter • Gary & Jen Walter • Fran Gladden • Bruce & Laura Avery • Clarissa Worley • Doug & Dawn Venn • Brant & Shellie Berglin • Shane & Darlene Anderson • Steve & Melissa Leddy • Matthew & Susan Gamble • Cleveland Hobdy • Dennis & Anita McKown • Wayne & Jeanine Kablanow •

DEDICATED

to the handful of leaders
I'm privileged to know
who stay awake at night
and dream about how
to honor God with their lives,
then start each day
with an unappeasable
passion to change the
world for Christ.

INTRODUCTION

*O*nly *those who throw away their lives for my sake and for the sake of the Good News will ever know what it means to really live.*

—Mark 8:35 (LB)

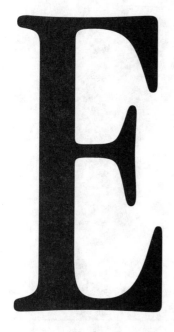

Every church stops growing when the price gets too high.

My wife and I were sightseeing in Moscow, Russia. Our guide was a bubbly, native-born woman who was proud of her city and eager to tell us all about it. We toured the Kremlin, stared at tourists kissing the tomb of Lenin, and smiled for a photo in front of St. Basil's cathedral.

Not far from the center of the city, Svetlana stopped at an old, abandoned building. One by one, its bricks were decomposing; its windows had long ago been plugged and barred. The heavy door – painted over who-knows-how-many times – was the only clue that people used to go inside. "This is an old church," her green glove pointed toward something that had once been important, "but it doesn't work anymore."

I admit I was puzzled. *The church doesn't work anymore?* We shuffled on to the next site without an explanation. Later that day, we entered one of Russia's finest churches. Chandeliers dripped from the ceiling. Candles burned as if they meant it. Muralled saints peered from the walls unrepentantly. A handful of older women worshiped with their hands folded and their heads covered with their scarves. Svetlana announced, "*This* is a working church."

Aha! I understood her lingo. A working church, to her, meant a church that was still in use. A church that didn't work anymore was dormant, boarded up, forsaken.

Let's consider our churches. What about a church that still opens its doors, yet has lost its purpose? Maybe it goes through all the right motions, but rarely reaches the lost for the kingdom. The lights are turned on, the organ still plays, but its era of growth is only a memory. Does Svetlana's declaration, "The church doesn't work anymore," have a meaning beyond a decaying building that begs to be demolished?

Most of our churches remain the same size year after year. Why? Can we blame our lack of growth on our message and on the harvest? Maybe our churches stay small because—hey! —we're the remnant; we're supposed to be small. Besides, so few people care about God these days. Perhaps our mission is to be faithful and to preserve what we already have.

The answer to all of the above is *No*. In Russian, the answer is *Nyet*. In Spanish it's *No*. In German, *Nein*. Whatever language you choose, the answer is the same. We cannot point the finger at our message or at the harvest to explain why most of our local churches remain the same size or get smaller year after year after year.

Churches stop growing for seven reasons which I have labeled habits. The purpose of this book is to demystify those reasons. Once you as a church leader understand what they are, you're in the position to make choices and sacrifices that matter. If you're willing, you can act in a way that will change your church from one that doesn't work anymore to a church that penetrates your community with living proof that God is love, Jesus is our Savior, and He is returning very soon.

The Culture of the Church

Not many people still make bread. Those who do have abandoned the old-fashioned method and instead pour the ingredients into an automatic bread machine. But everyone knows the answer to this question: What happens if you're making bread, you put all the right ingredients together, knead it just right, bake it for precisely the right time at the right temperature—but you forget to add the yeast? You have bricks. Or bookends. Or door stops.

A church can do all the right things, but if it doesn't have the right yeast or the right culture, everything else will make little or no difference. Let's say you understand the seven habits and your church does everything right. But if the culture is bad, the bread of life will be stale, hard, and barely edible. So before we dive into the habits themselves, we have to create the right culture.

Culture can be defined as the traditions, symbols, values, acceptable behaviors, ideals, language, customs and meaning that depict a unified way of life. Every organization—including the church—has its own unique culture. Like yeast, it's almost invisible, but it is very, very real. It affects everything. The culture of your church shapes personal relationships, determines church priorities, and impacts short- and long-term plans. In short, it makes or breaks everything else you do.

I spend a lot of time on airplanes; I'm on 125-150 flights a year. Fortunately, I'm not afraid of flying. Sometimes, the plane will land and I'm so immersed in a book that I don't even notice. All too often, however, I run across people who are terrified. John Madden, the sometimes-obnoxious commentator of Monday Night Football, rides the bus for thousands of miles between games rather than face his fear of flying. Others, in a conscious act of bravery, stumble aboard muttering "if I perish, I perish," and resign themselves to accept their fate.

On a recent flight, a teenage girl across the aisle from me was so afraid that she vomited over and over. I felt awful for her (not to mention the man seated next to her who never did get to eat his meal). When the flight was over, her skin was green. She could hardly walk off the plane of her own accord.

I once sat next to a woman who was so afraid of flying that she asked if I would hold her hand while we flew. My brain handed me one excuse after the other, but I finally agreed and I held this strange lady's hand. When I got home, my wife wanted to know how old she was. "Really old," I assured her. "How old is really old?" She was genuinely curious. She almost insisted on a birth certificate.

Another time I was seated next to a gentleman who was obviously terrified. He was sweating like a blacksmith in August; he clawed the window; he struggled to breathe. "Are you afraid of flying?" I asked the obvious question.

"I'm petrified," he admitted.

"You'll be fine," I assured him. "I do this all the time and I've never had any problem."

I asked where he was from, about his line of work, how many children he had, what his hobbies were, but nothing seemed to help. Then he asked me what I do for a living.

"I'm a minister," I answered.

"Like a pastor?" he asked.

"Yes, sir."

He literally threw his hands into the air and exclaimed, "Praise the Lord! Now I know I'm safe!" as if ministers are excused from plane crashes.

There's a reason I'm not afraid of flying. In fact, I'm not afraid of much of anything. I recently leaped out of an airplane at 12,000 feet—voluntarily—and free-fell over a mile down to 5,000 feet. It was 45 seconds of pure bliss! The reason I'm not afraid is simple. If I fall out of the sky someday, it's OK. I don't want to, but if I do, it's OK. Because if I die in a plane crash, the very next thing I will see is Jesus coming in the clouds to take me home. Not because I deserve it by any stretch of the mind, but because each day I devote my life to Him and I start each day with the blessed assurance of eternal life.

But what about the people on the plane who don't know Jesus? It's not OK if they perish in a plane crash without the hope of eternal life.

So here's a question. Why would we do church for people who already have that hope? Sure, we ourselves need church. The writer of Hebrews admonishes us to "forsake not the assembling of ourselves together."[1] We need the blessing of worshipping God corporately, of connecting with one another and refreshing our faith. But the primary purpose of our churches is not to meet *our* needs and the needs of our children. It's to continue the work of Him who came to seek to save the lost, to coalesce our energies and resources to make sure that—whatever it takes—as many people as possible end up in God's kingdom.

Your church needs a strong culture in four areas. It won't possess that culture naturally; those who lead the church must be deliberate and persistent in creating and protecting that culture in these four areas.

Outreach

At the opening ceremony for Disney World, Walt Disney, the creative genius behind the theme park, declared, "We didn't build this for ourselves. We built it for others."[2]

The church does not exist for the sake of the church. It exists to continue the work of the One who came to seek to save the lost. Many churches have forgotten why the church exists. And you can feel it when you walk in. There's no passion, no energy, no concern for those without Christ.

I know of a pastor who begins every board meeting by doing something strange. He lays a newspaper on the table in front of the board members and opens it to the obituary page. "These are the people in our community who died the last few days," he announces. "Look at their faces. Read their names. Some of them were probably ready for heaven. Most of them were not. Are we as a church going to try and change that for the thousands of people in our town who are still alive?" It might be an odd way to begin a board meeting, but it works. It reminds everyone that if they end up in heaven but the people in their community don't, it's not OK.

Another church has labeled the benches in their lobby "Fools Benches." Here's why. From day one, the leaders have urged the members to invite their unsaved friends to church. Most of the members try it. They invite a neighbor or someone they work with to visit the church. They sit on the benches in the lobby waiting for their friend to arrive. You know that when people say they will come, sometimes they do and sometimes they don't. The member sits on the bench waiting and praying and hoping; if the friend doesn't come, they waited for nothing—and they feel like a fool. So everyone refers to the benches as "Fools Benches" because virtually everyone has experienced it and everyone is willing to be a fool for Jesus.

There are some things you don't need to pray about. You don't need to pray about whether or not the church should pray. You don't need to pray about whether or not the church should serve. And you don't need to pray about whether or not the church should evangelize.

Rick Warren asserts that Christians forget the purpose of the church every 26 days. If they are not repeatedly and constantly reminded, they drift into the default position which is the view that church is for the already convinced. (The time period of 26 days comes from the era of Nehemiah when Israel was rebuilding Jerusalem's wall and they lost their original vision.)

Jesus' last words before His return to heaven were, "You are my witnesses." There is no such thing as an inward-focused church. The very term is an oxymoron. The purpose of the church is not up for grabs. God doesn't give us a coin and say, "Heads, do church for yourselves; tails, prioritize the lost." The core value is this: "Our highest calling is to passionately seek to save the lost."

It's up to the pastor and the other leaders to create and nourish the culture of outreach, to make decisions based on what will help us reach the next lost person. It's up to church leaders to focus every resource, every energy, every spiritual gift on the task of continuing the ministry of the One who came to seek the lost.

Commitment

Mahatma Ghandi, known as the father of India, studied the teachings of Jesus and once said, "You Christians look after a document containing enough dynamite to blow all civilization to pieces, turn the world upside down and bring peace to a battle-torn planet. But you treat it as though it is nothing more than a piece of good literature."[3]

The second element of the yeast or culture is that of commitment. Here's the core value: "Full devotion to Christ and His cause is normal for every believer." Your church can make a difference only by creating and maintaining a culture of high expectations, where those who follow Christ are willing—even eager—to serve Him according to their spiritual maturity and their spiritual gifts.

The unemployment rate in most churches is frightening. The pastor and a few of the members knock themselves out in an all-out effort to keep the church afloat, but the majority are uninvolved. In high-commitment churches, it is normal to serve. When members come to the game, they don't head for the bleachers to watch someone else carry the ball. They head for the field where they consider it an honor to be a player, to contribute to the greatest cause God ever gave humankind.

In fact, research proves that high-commitment churches are the ones that are growing. In his excellent book *Surprising Insights from the Unchurched,* Thom Rainer says, "The unchurched are more likely to return if they understand the church expects much of their members."[4] By contrast, low-commitment churches—some people call them "church-lite"—struggle to pay the bills and preserve status quo.

The defining symbol of the church is the cross. Jesus instructed Christians to take it up and He tied high commitment to following Him. It's all too easy for the church to abandon the cross and to allow serving to become a take-it-or-leave-it option. A few find themselves bearing the burdens while the rest either cheer them on, sit passively, or sometimes even target them with criticism. It's up to the pastor and the other leaders to create and protect the culture of commitment, to build high expectations in appropriate ways, to establish the climate and the structures where—hey!—everyone who hangs out around here gets to serve according to their spiritual maturity and their spiritual gifts."

Fun

Third, your church needs a strong culture of fun. Here's a question: Why would you invite someone to attend church if you yourself don't enjoy it? If you find it boring, you'd have to be threatened, shamed or bribed to get up the courage to invite your neighbor. The core value is this: "Boredom violates biblical principle and creates spiritual apathy." In appropriate ways, church should be fun.

According to the movie *Pollyanna*, there are 826 texts in the Bible that tell us to have fun. Whether or not the count in the movie is accurate is not the point. There are hundreds of texts that tell us to have fun, to be joyful, to rejoice. And not one of them implies that fun is illegal on Sabbath or in the worship experience. C.S. Lewis asserts that "joy is the serious business of heaven."[5] Show me a church that is reaching the lost, and I'll show you a church where people are having fun.

I think we've been confused. We know about the wall of separation between church and state—may that wall stand firm! Someone, however, pawned off on us the notion that we need a wall of separation between church and fun. Not so. A friend of mine paraphrases an Old Testament passage to read, "Where the Spirit of the Lord is, there is fun!" For a church to be positioned to penetrate its community, church leaders must deliberately create a cheerful climate of joy—yes, even fun—in the church.

Prayer

Fourth, the church lives in the culture of prayer. You are not selling health insurance or managing a Starbucks. You are leading and shaping the Church of the living God. The pastor and church leaders must create the culture of prayer by constantly putting everything into eternal perspective and calling for dependence on God. The core value is: "God has promised His blessing on those who ask."

Solomon offers that perspective when he says, "The horse is prepared for battle, but deliverance is of the Lord."[6] When it's time for battle, who prepares the horse? It's not God. He won't throw on the saddle and position the bit. When the enemy approaches, it's up to you and to me to get the horse ready. Once you have done your part, God shows up and deliverance is certain. If you sleep in on the day of battle and wait for God to prepare the horse, you're in trouble. If, on the other hand, you get up before dawn and charge headlong into the fray of conflict without God, you will taste of humiliation and defeat.

The same balance emerges when you compare Matthew 16:18 with Matthew 28:19, 20. In the first text, Jesus says, "I will do it. I will build My church." In the second, He tells us, "You do it. Go and make disciples." Whose responsibility is it, His or ours? The answer is 'yes.' We work in harmony with practical and proven principles, we act as wisely and diligently as we can, then God does what only God can do: He shows His sovereignty and builds His church.

Nehemiah never prayed for God to rebuild Jerusalem's broken-down wall. He prayed, instead, for an opportunity to go rebuild it himself—with God's blessing. What is the difference between a dreamer who prays and a visionary who prays? A dreamer prays that things will be different. A visionary prays that God will use him or her to make a difference in obedience to God's call.

In the church, prayer is first an attitude that undergirds and permeates everything. It's the breath of the church. It's a spoken and unspoken recognition that we're neck deep in a spiritual struggle between the forces of good and the forces of evil. But beyond attitude, the church that takes its task seriously makes prayer an ongoing priority in the schedule of the church—in tangible ways—so that every member has the chance to enter God's presence and experience God's mighty acts.

Remember, every church stops growing when the price gets too high. Or, as one person warned, every plateau eventually ends in a cliff. So before you read any further, enthusiastically embrace the four elements that comprise a healthy culture. Then devote yourself to understanding the seven reasons why so many churches make such a short-term evangelistic impact. Finally, make the decision that whatever price your church must pay, you and your fellow leaders will pay it—for the sake of the lost, for the sake of Christ, for the sake of the kingdom.

Are you ready? Are you serious? Are you sure? Let's go.

---

1   Hebrews 10:25.

2   Walt Kallestad, *Turn Your Church Inside Out*, p. 18.

3   Challenge Weekly, <u>chalpub@iconz.co.nz</u>, and cited in Friday Fax, 31 July 1997.

4   Page 111.

5   *Letters to Malcolm*, p. 93.

6   Proverbs 21:31.

HABIT

THE PASTOR

It is the pastors and church leaders who are willing to do what other pastors and church leaders are afraid or unwilling to do who will change the world.

—Adam Hamilton

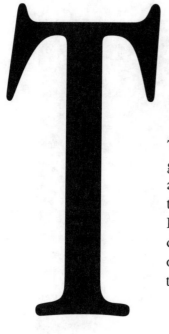

The first reason many churches stop growing is the pastor. Pardon me for alienating all of the pastors so early in the book, but it's undeniably true. Pastors are often the reason that churches remain the same size from one year to the next. Read on and I think you'll agree.

The Pastor's Role

Most Adventist pastors do not function Biblically. They have been taught—and the pressure is on—to personally care for every member. Once they accept that as their role, they assure that the church will remain small. After all, how many families can the pastor serve? How many evenings does he have to visit? How many hours are in the day?

Several years ago, I was serving in the upper Midwest. My job description was half-time ministerial director for the conference and half-time pastor of two churches: a church plant in the capitol city and an old church ten miles beyond the boondocks.

The old church opened in 1861—two years before the General Conference was organized—and it still meets in its original building. To get to the church, turn onto Advent Road, follow a curve, and there it is on the left. The church boasts its own cemetery where half-drowned gravestones—including that of a GC president—peer out of the earth like sleepy spectators at a long-winded revival.

In theory, I spent half of my time *with* the pastors and half *being* a pastor. On the first Sabbath of every month, I preached in the little church in the country at 9:30 a.m. As soon as the sermon was over—sometimes even during the closing song— I jumped in my diesel Volkswagen and pleaded with the anemic engine to hurry me back to town so I could preach in the new church.

One Sabbath, I was in the little church. The deacon was collecting the offering while the organ and piano performed a duet. Before the music stopped, one of the saints stood to her feet and flung a verbal grenade in my direction. "Pastor, we don't think you come to our church often enough! Once a month is too seldom. We expect you to be here more often. Understand me clearly. This is *not* negotiable!" The expression on her face was stronger than her words.

Sixty eyes stared straight ahead. Thirty tongues were silent. I stepped to the mike and smiled. "I want to thank you, Sister, for your nice comments. I love coming to this church, and to hear you say that you want me to come even more often than I do is very affirming. I wish I could be here more often. If I wasn't so busy, I'd come here every week. I'm not able to, but thank you so much for the nice words. I really love you folks, too." I sat down. Case closed, right? Guess again.

Later that week, the dear sister called the conference office and spoke with my president. He called me into his office. The proverbial mouse in the corner heard the following: "Ron,

I got a call from one of the leaders at the little church. They're wondering if you can come down and preach more often, maybe twice a month instead of once. I told them I'd talk with you, so what do you think?"

You know what he expected me to say, but I couldn't say it. Instead, I answered: "Every time I say *Yes*, I say *No*. If I say *Yes* to this, I have to say *No* to something else. I already work as hard as I can. Which do you want me to do, spend less time with the pastors in the conference, or less time in my church plant?"

"Oh, I don't know, Ron. But the members down there are such precious people. Don't you think you could squeeze them into your schedule just one more time a month?"

I shook my head before I spoke. "*No*. The answer is *No*. If I do, I'll neglect the pastors and the church plant won't grow. I love them, and I definitely respect you, but the answer is *No*."

Fortunately, the president swallowed hard and accepted my answer. It helped, no doubt, that I was ordained and I had recently received several calls.

Many churches have ceased their cycle of growth for this reason alone. When I say that the pressure is on for the pastor to himself care for every need in the church, I'm as serious as Stalin. It's a rare pastor who (a) understands his or her role, (b) has the courage to say *No* when the members and the conference leaders insist that they personally serve every member, and (c) actually says *Yes* to the things that grow a church.

Serving as half-time ministerial director, while pastoring two churches, forced me to clarify my role. I took advantage of the fact that everyone knew I couldn't possibly do everything a pastor is normally expected to do and I wrote my own job description. Yours will no doubt be different, but here's what

I wrote and what was accepted by both the church board and the church in business session:

(1) Be an authentic, spiritual person

(2) Lead worship as often as possible

(3) Be a leader of leaders (organize teams for ministry)

(4) Model one-on-one friendship evangelism

(5) Be the church's primary vision-caster and spiritual counselor

The list doesn't include a number of things pastors normally do. My leaders agreed, however, that if I did those five things well, the church would grow. And it did.

Missing from this list is hospital visitation. I wasn't able to do it very often. So I told the members that our Care Unit ministry would make our hospital visitations. "If you end up in the hospital," I assured them publicly, "I guarantee that you'll be well visited. But I won't be able to come myself unless you're really in bad shape."

One morning I had worship at the church school. One of our members was in a nearby hospital for something routine so I decided to pop in and have prayer with her. When she saw my face she panicked. She thought she must have some dreadful condition or else I wouldn't have appeared in her room. It wasn't long until the members expected a member to visit them instead of me—and not only were they fine with that, they actually preferred it—because they knew I was working hard to build ministry teams and reach the lost. I learned that if a pastor loves God, loves the people and works hard, the members will cut him or her a lot of slack.

Years ago, someone asked HMS Richards, Sr. how to finish the work. His answer is a classic: "Put all the preachers in jail. The work will never be done," he asserted, "until the laymen rally to the cause, but the laymen won't do it until the preachers get out of the way."

The Bible is clear. The role of the pastor is to "Equip the saints for the work of the ministry."[7] Not to *do* the work of the ministry, but to equip *the members* to do the work of the ministry. When pastors function the way God intended, everyone wins because more people end up serving and more of the lost find Christ. If a pastor functions unbiblically, his or her arrest might actually propel the work forward in that particular city!

In Acts 6, a mini-crisis erupted in the church. The church was growing so fast that the twelve apostles could no longer personally care for everyone's needs. The widows were upset. One of them may even have stood to complain during the Sabbath morning offering. The apostles called a business meeting. The members were instructed to organize to meet the needs of the congregation, while the apostles led out in prayer and in ministering the Word. The result was fantastic: "And the word of God spread, and the number of the disciples multiplied greatly in Jerusalem."[8]

Consider a serious question: What if the role of the apostles had not changed? What if they had acquiesced to their conference president's wishes? What if they had agreed to continue to personally serve every member? The results would have been tragic. The phenomenal moving of God would never have happened. The church in Jerusalem would have plateaued with the members convinced that they must have reached all the interested people in their town—while the apostles teetered on the verge of burnout.

Whenever a pastor functions Biblically, the number of disciples increases (assuming the other "church habits" are in place). That's why the role of the pastor is so foundational. Remember, in the parable of the lost sheep, Jesus praises the shepherd who leaves the 99 and goes out searching for the one lost sheep.[9]

Imagine that you're driving a car with a manual transmission. Put the car in first gear, release the clutch, and race the engine. What happens? You travel down the road at—what?—15 miles an hour. This is how most pastors function. They have their pedal to the metal but they're not accomplishing much. They race their engine. They pin their RPM needle to the max. They measure their effectiveness by how often they neglect their family, their health, and their devotional life. On the verge of burning up their engine, they plead with their conference, "If you'd only give me an associate pastor, we could accomplish so much more." If the conference can afford to, they assign another pastor to the church and now two pastors lurch down the freeway in first gear at 15 miles an hour.

What is second gear? Turning over ministry to people in the church. Allowing people to use their God-given passion and spiritual gifts to serve. Organizing so that everyone gets a chance to contribute to the spread of the gospel.

Third gear? More of the same. As the church reaches different levels of attendance, the pastor makes a conscious move from functioning as a shepherd to serving as a rancher. The shepherd personally cares for all of the sheep. A rancher sees that all the sheep are cared for, but he does not personally care for them himself. Like the apostles of Acts 6, he organizes the church so that he is no longer a leader of followers, but a leader of leaders.[10]

If you are a pastor, ask yourself this question: *Do I spend my time on a typical day the same way Bill Hybels does?* (Hybels pastors a church where somewhere around 20,000 people attend every week.) I think I can predict your answer. Now ask an even more important question: *Do I spend my time the same way Hybels did when he had the same number of members I have today?* Most of the time the answer is *No.* If Bill Hybels had functioned like a typical Adventist pastor when his church was small, it would be small to this day. Every Adventist church needs a sign between the lobby and the worship center that says, "The pastor and his wife are not omnipresent. Let them serve Biblically."

Ellen White pulls no punches. "It weakens those who know the truth for our ministers to expend on them the time and talent that should be given to the unconverted."[11] We don't often admit it out loud, but our tradition of insisting that the pastor personally serves the needs of the members has resulted in their spiritual weakness. Not to mention the loss of multiplied thousands of souls who could have and should have found Christ.

The easiest way to clarify the pastor's role is to ask this question: Who is our number one constituency? Is it (a) current members and their children, or (b) those who will not go to heaven unless something changes between now and Jesus' coming? The apostles' answer in Acts 6 was clear. Ours must be, too.

The Pastor's Gift Mix

The role of a pastor, what he or she actually does day-by-day, is foundational. But if a pastor is to lead the church to grow, he or she must be strong in three competencies. The first is **leadership**.

A famous leadership guru asserts that leadership is influence. More specifically, it is a cultivated influence that you come to have in people's lives. Peter Drucker states the obvious: "There is only one characteristic common to all leaders: Followers."[12] Yet most pastors function more like a chaplain than a leader. They emerge from seminary trained to care for people and to preach, not necessarily to lead.

One pastor told me—somewhat tongue-in-cheek, I hope— that as a pastor, he feels like the overseer in a cemetery; he has lots of people under him, but no one is following! Maybe they aren't following because he isn't leading. "He who thinketh he leadeth, and hath no one following," John Maxwell reminds us, "is only taking a walk."

Christian researcher George Barna discovered a startling fact. "Three out of four American pastors do not believe they are called, gifted or skilled as leaders."[13] Perhaps the gift of leadership was less important when the majority of people lived in rural areas and rode to church on or behind a horse. The pastor could be a chaplain to the dozen families in the church and everything was just fine.

Today, the pastor of a growing church is not just a manager; he cannot just keep the machinery running smoothly. He must lead. His mandate is to step up and take the initiative so that the church makes a serious impact on its community.

Take leadership away from a church and it isn't long until confusion replaces vision, morale erodes, and enthusiasm fades. The whole vision morphs from a focused passion to reach the lost into a desperate effort to preserve what God gave the church many years ago.

What does a leader do? He devises and nurtures an environment in which people believe they can make a dent in the universe. He stays awake at night, pounds his pillow and pleads with God for inspiration and instruction about what to do to grow the kingdom. As God's vision begins to take shape in his mind, he shares it with people he trusts and carefully weighs their response. Once the vision is clear, he paints a picture of a desirable future, then inspires and organizes people so they step into that picture.

If a pastor is not a leader, he or she must *become* a leader. Leadership is rarely granted at birth. It is nurtured and grown by someone who feels an irrevocable call to make a difference. Pastors who believe that God will be glorified when their church reaches the lost will read leadership books, watch leadership tapes, attend leadership conferences, and hang out with exceptional leaders.[14]

The pastor must also be strong in a second gift: **Evangelism**. I don't mean public evangelism, although that ability is certainly a plus. Pastors who lead growing churches actually enjoy spending time one-on-one with secular people. They have an affinity with the unchurched. They model personal evangelism. They share their stories and teach others how to build redemptive friendships.

A pastor who talks about personal evangelism but does not do it himself will never lead a church that reaches the lost. A pastor who spends virtually all of his time with the saints will never lead a church that reaches the lost.

Just as important as leadership and evangelism to a pastor's gift mix is that of **communication**. Churches that grow *always* have excellent preaching. *Strategies for Today's Leader* magazine asked pastors in evangelistically effective churches, "What excites you most about ministry?" Ninety percent said preaching.[15] If the pastor is not excited about preaching, the people are not excited about listening.

I was leading a seminar in a Midwestern Adventist church. "What is the largest church in town?" I asked the audience. Several people quickly named the church. "Why do you think it has grown so large?" I asked.

A hand went up in the back. "It's the music!" An older lady spit out the words with a level of energy that startled everyone.

"Really?" I said. "What kind of music do they do?"

"It's awful!" she said. "And that's why they grow!" Her mind was narrower than Roy Rogers' tie.

"Let's test that theory," I suggested. "Do you think there are any other churches in this city that use the same kind of music but they have not grown?"

"Hmmm," the crowd murmured. Heads bobbed up and down.

"Then it's not the music."

What is it? A combination of things contribute to the continual growth of a church, all of which will be discussed in this book. But one common ingredient that you will *always, always, always* find is strong preaching. Without it, the finest and most committed group of leaders will preside over a church that struggles to grow. Please don't panic and think *Well, our church is sunk. We'll never have strong preaching.* I'll let you know in a future chapter exactly how virtually anyone can become an excellent preacher. Really!

Tenure

Your church can't grow very big if the pastor doesn't function Biblically. If he or she is weak in leadership, evangelism or communication, you're facing an enormous challenge. But there's another issue that often negates all the good things that happen in a church. It's tenure. How long the pastor stays.

A few years ago, I took "Church Growth I" from C. Peter Wagner at Fuller Seminary. The class discussion drifted onto the topic of pastoral tenure. When his face cracked into a huge smile, we all expected one of Wagner's unforgettable jokes. "Listen to this!" he said. "Seventh-day Adventist pastors move so often that many of their conferences actually own moving vans to move the pastors around!" The class roared as if Wagner was making it up just to get a laugh. It took several attempts to convince the students that it's actually true.

Imagine a family that gets a new father every few years. What kind of family does that produce? A dysfunctional family. Now imagine a church that gets a new pastor every few years. What kind of church does that produce? Evangelistically, it assures a dysfunctional church.

Most Adventist pastors do not feel called to the church where they serve. They are only there because the higher bidder hasn't called yet. They are "called" where they are until the phone rings with an invitation to serve a bigger church, move "up" to the conference office, the *Adventist Review* or the college. John Knox said, "Give me Scotland or I die!" Few Adventist pastors feel so strongly called to their town that they are willing to devote a major portion of their lives to building up the church in that city. Amazingly, some conference presidents actually believe that short pastorates are good for the church.

The word "tenure" literally means "ten years." Ten years is the normal horizon of human activities, the time we take to educate a child, the time required to establish a business. Ten years is also the outer limit of political predictability. In ten years, governments change, political leaders rise and fall, empires collapse, wars and revolutions turn the world upside down.

If the other factors are in place—which means the pastor functions Biblically and has the proper gift mix—a pastor who stays ten years makes ten times the difference compared to a pastor who stays three or four years. Permanent change virtually never happens in an established church in less than ten years. Do the research and you'll find that there is a direct correlation between the size of the church and how long the pastor stays. With the exception of an institutional church, the larger the church, the longer the pastor stays. The smaller the church, the more frequently the pastor moves.

What do you do when the telephone rings and you're invited to pastor in greener pastures? Remember and repeat the slogan that has kept one pastor in his church for many years: "Veni, Vedi, Velcro—I came, I saw, I stuck around."[16] God uses those who ignore the calls to "move up higher" to make a much greater difference for the kingdom.

Staffing

One of the most complicated issues for conference leaders is staffing a church for growth.

A church planter recently urged me to twist his conference president's arm and get him an associate pastor. "Why should he?" I asked.

"Because I'm totally maxed out. If I had some help, my church would grow."

"What makes you think so?" I taunted him.

"We've grown to 150 in attendance," he said. "We have two services on Sabbath, I'm working my tail off and I just can't do anymore."

"Make a list of the last five churches in your conference that have added an associate pastor," I suggested. "Then track their growth. What do you think you'll find?"

He knew I had him. He felt as frustrated as a crab in a Safeway aquarium.

I was only playing devil's advocate; I really was on his side. I knew how he functioned—his leadership transmission was already in third or fourth gear—and I shared his confidence that the right associate would help take his church to the next level. But I had to prepare him for his president's response.

Put your finger on a map. I don't care what state or province you point to. Show me a North American city and I'll show you an Adventist church that has plateaued many years ago. Add another pastor to that church and the church will not grow. Add five pastors to that church and the church will not grow. Why? Because the leaders of the church have been unaware of—or have ignored—one or more of the other reasons why churches stop growing. Fix those reasons, then add the right staff person at the right time, and the church will most definitely be propelled to greater growth.[17] But whatever you do, don't miss this: Not adding staff at the right time will make certain that your church is done growing, even if you do everything else right.

So the first reason why a church stops growing is the pastor. If he tries to personally care for all of the members' needs, if he is weak in one or more of the three competencies, or if he bounces from church to church too frequently, he himself will be the reason why the church plateaus. And remember, every church stops growing when the price gets too high.

Now hang on as we discover the other six reasons why churches stop growing.

---

7   Ephesians 4:11.

8   Acts 6:1-7.

9   Luke 15:4-7.

10   See Gary McIntosh, *One Size Doesn't Fit All,* for an outstanding explanation of the pastor's role at each stage of growth.

11   Ellen White, *Testimonies,* Vol. 7, p. 18. Also read the entire chapter titled "Working for Church Members".

12   Peter Drucker, *Strategies for Today's Leader,* 2nd Quarter, 2002, p. 20.

13   Barna Update, 1-16-01.

14   John Maxwell declares that five percent of leaders become leaders as a result of a crisis, ten percent because of natural gifting, and 85 percent due to the influence of other leaders. (See *The 21 Irrefutable Laws of Leadership,* p. 133.)

15   *Strategies for Today's Leader,* 1st Quarter, 2001, p. 11.

16   Steve Sjogren, *Community of Kindness,* p. 80.

17   For an outstanding explanation of the staffing issues, read *Staff Your Church for Growth* by Gary McIntosh.

HABIT

2

THE FACILITY

*W*e control the initial decision as to where we
will meet. But from that point on, our location
controls us. Be sure you are controlled in a manner
that ensures rather than hinders growth.

—Ralph Moore

The second reason many churches stop growing is the facility. This one doesn't sound very spiritual, but read along and I'm sure you'll agree.

▪ The Living Room

Let's suppose that you decide to plant a church in your town. A few folks embrace the vision and you start laying plans. One of the big decisions is where you will meet. "We have a large living room," one of the saints offers. "Why not start meeting there?" You scratch your head and decide, "Sure! Jerry and Jenny's house would be perfect."

Services begin with a dozen people. Twelve grows to twenty, then thirty. Everyone is jammed into the living room, shoulder to shoulder—you couldn't get another soul into the room without stacking people up—but they've never enjoyed church more in their lives.

One Sabbath, Jerry says out loud what everyone is thinking. "I love our new, little church. And I really like the cozy feel of the living room. If we move out of here someday, we'll lose the intimacy, the family feel, the love. Jenny and I have talked it over and we're glad to open our home every single Sabbath. So we insist that we never, ever move out of our living room. In fact, I'll make a motion. Until Jesus comes, this church will always meet in this living room." The motion is quickly seconded, and in a unanimous gush of emotions, everyone agrees.

What have you just decided? You're done growing. You can mail a flyer to every home in the county, spend thousands on a reaping series, distribute Discover Bible lessons far and wide, and help every smoker within 20 miles kick the habit, but your church will not grow. Your facility has limited your vision.

The Church Building

Let's agree that's not acceptable. You have to think bigger than that. Especially in light of the fact that within a Frisbee toss of the house are thousands of lost people. So instead, you think bigger. You dream; you sacrifice; you tap the Union revolving fund and erect a church that seats, say, two hundred people. You are exceptionally proud of your church! But when you move in, the unspoken assumption is that *this is the place where the Adventist church will meet in this town until Jesus comes.*

What have you just decided? The same thing as before. The number is different, but once you approach capacity, you're done growing. The physical realities of your church have limited your vision.[18]

We have just placed our finger on a serious problem. A couple of decades after World War II, American Adventists had the money to build new churches. Pay a visit to just about any city in North America and you'll find an Adventist church that was built in the '60s or '70s. There are a few exceptions, but not many. Those churches range in size from a hundred seats to five or six hundred. When they were built, several things were true.

First, we believed that Jesus was coming in 10-15 years, so the unstated assumption was that *this is the place where the Adventist church will meet until Jesus returns.* It was never recorded in the business meeting minutes, but everyone assumed that *our new church is sufficient in this town until the end of time.* And woe to the person—then or now—who has the audacity to suggest that we relocate!

Second, churches don't hold as many people as they used to. If you were a church architect in the '60s, you would plan on 70 people for every 100 running feet of pews. Today's architects plan on 52 people for the same 100 feet of pews.[19] Why? Ask the Surgeon General (or look in the mirror!). Churches that were designed to hold 200 persons now accommodate 150 or so.

▦ The Parking Lot

Third, our parking lots are grossly inadequate. Wind the clock back to the '70s. It's Sabbath morning and you've decided to count the attendance. You add up the people at church, divide by the number of cars, and find that four people come to church per car. The reality is that many families only had one car in the '70s. Some families didn't have a car at all so they called you to come and pick them up. The average car brought four people to church.[20]

> Q: How many off-street parking places do we need?
>
> A: What year is it?
>
> 1940 – none or few
>
> 1970 – one for every 4 seats
>
> Today – one for every 2 seats
>
> 2025 – who knows?

Stand in the church parking lot today. Count the people, divide by the number of cars, and you'll count two persons per car.[21] Why? For one thing, most American families have two, three or even four cars. Our family of four has been known to take four cars to church on Sabbath. Also, our society consists of many more singles than in years past. Calculate the bodies that crawl out of cars on Sabbath morning and you'll count fewer than two. The cruel reality is, if you can't park people, you won't need to.

The Shopping Mall

Let me use the mall to illustrate the importance of adequate parking. I'm not really a shopper. "Shop until you drop" sounds like punishment to me. When Christmas or a birthday rolls around, I log onto the Internet, make a few clicks and— *poof!*—the merchandise magically shows up at my door within a few days. Why drive clear across town and waste gas and time when a website and credit card can accomplish the same thing? And the absolute worst day to shop is one of the busiest shopping days of the year—the day after Thanksgiving.

My wife is the opposite. When the newspaper comes Thanksgiving week, she examines the inserts with evangelistic zeal. She cuts out the ads, circles the specials, lists the sizes and quantities, then charts out her itinerary as if planning a tour of Peru.

Last year, tragedy struck. She had to work the day after Thanksgiving and I had the day off. It seemed perfectly logical, she decided, that I should represent her at store after store after store. The crowds were awful. People snarled at total strangers to get ahead in line. Normally docile citizens cursed one another when deprived of "their" parking space. I spent more time idling in traffic and standing in line than actually shopping. I eventually found most everything on the list, but I came home in an emotional slump.

I started to think: What if a mall had seven parking places? What kind of business would they do without adequate parking? Now imagine a church with seven parking places.

■ The Church with Seven Parking Places

I was asked to spend a weekend in Fargo, North Dakota. The pastor invited me to help them discover why the church hadn't grown in many years. I flew to Fargo on Friday, rented a car, and drove to the church on Sabbath morning. From the time the tire of my car rolled onto the church property, it took me 0.7 seconds to diagnose the problem. There were seven parking places. It's possible to park some cars on the street, but not very many.

Here's a quiz: Who arrives at church first, members or guests? And where do the members park? Two blocks away so that guests can have the seven parking spaces? Don't you wish.

Our afternoon meeting was lively. I poured a cup full of water and said, "This cup represents your parking lot. Let's suppose we want it to hold more water—what shall we do? How about if we pour with *more enthusiasm* than ever before? What will happen? The cup runneth over. Let's decide to pour with a *purer motive* than ever before. Will the cup hold more water now?" And then I really got their attention. "How about if we pray—and then pour? Will the cup hold more water?" The silence would have depressed a monk.

"Let's be real," I jolted them out of their shock. "If God wanted to, He could no doubt make the cup hold more water. But don't expect Him to if another cup stands nearby." They got the point. They had been praying, but their prayer was, essentially, a plea for God to make their already-full cup hold more water.

I hear it all the time. "Maybe if we pray more," someone says, "God will make our church grow in spite of everything else." He could, but Ellen White advises us not to use prayer as a substitute for common sense. "God does not generally work miracles to advance His truth," she writes. "He works according to great principles made known to us, and it is our part to mature wise plans and set in operation the means whereby God shall bring about certain results."[22]

The Church with Ninety Parking Places

The Fargo story was repeated in another town. At the pastor's request, I flew in on Friday, then showed up on Sabbath to help the leaders find out why attendance was half what it had been twenty years before. Before Sabbath School started, I was out in the parking lot counting spaces. There were ninety. My previous research revealed that the average Sabbath attendance in 1980 was 360. Two decades later, about 185 were in church each week. During those twenty years, the church had been led by some outstanding pastors. Several evangelists had come to town and baptized scores of people. So why had attendance fallen so severely?

Once again, our afternoon meeting was lively. I asked them three questions:

(a) How many off-street parking spaces do you have?

(b) How many people came to church per car in 1980?

(c) How many people come to church per car today?

Let's do the math. Ninety parking spaces times 4 people per car equals 360, exactly the attendance in 1980. Ninety parking spaces times 2 people per car equals 180, very close to their attendance today.

I filled the cup with water, read Ellen White's quotation, and flashed these words on the screen: "Every church stops growing when the price gets too high." Then I outlined their price.

"Your first choice is to buy homes around the church at $200,000 each, knock them down, and pave the lots. And your church will grow.

"Second, you can go to two worship services on Sabbath to double the use of your space. You'll grow. But be aware that double services almost never outlast the pastor who started them (except on an institutional campus). So Option Two is a temporary fix unless your pastor is here for the long haul." (He is already gone, so that wouldn't have been a good choice.)

"Third, you can relocate. Find ten or twenty acres and build another church."

"Fourth, you can plant a church. Send away ten or twenty percent of your active members and within 18 months, your attendance and giving will be right back where they were. Meanwhile, across town, your new church will reach lost people who will never be won to Christ in this church." They voted that afternoon to plant a church. I'm delighted to tell you that the planter is already on site.

Indeed, a strange phenomenon exists in North America: When people come to church, they bring their cars. If you don't care about their cars, you don't care about them.

A while back I presented the Seven Habits at a pastors' meeting. After discussing how facilities often stifle growth, a pastor stood to his feet. "Ron," he blurted out with energy, "My church seats 300 but we only have 50 places to park. You're right about two people coming to church per car; our attendance has hovered around 100 for several years now. But we have no way to expand our parking lot. You're telling me that we can't grow unless we do something about it. Come on, man, give me some hope!"

I gave him some hope. "I hope you'll realize," I said with the biggest smile I could muster, "that if you can't park people you won't need to. I hope you'll remember that every church stops growing when the price gets too high. And I hope you'll decide that because the lost matter to God, you will pay whatever price you must to reach them for the kingdom. Unless you do, you are, for the most part, squandering your programs, your plans and your prayers." His face told me he got it but he swallowed his words.

In John 6:60, Jesus was speaking on a different topic. When He paused to catch His breath, His disciples shook their heads and announced, "This is a hard saying!" Many church leaders say the same about 21st century church facilities: This is a hard saying. It is not easy or cheap to fix the problem. But Spirit-filled leaders don't seek easy or cheap solutions. Their singular question is: *What do we have to do to reach the lost? Once we know, we will do it.*

Whether it's a living room that holds thirty or a parking lot built for seven, all the good things you do are limited by the physical reality of your facility. Because your facility defines your vision.

The Attractiveness of Your Church Building

I was guest preacher in a large, urban church. When I drove up, I was disappointed to find the grounds untended and the gutter falling off the roof. Then I saw the sign. Not the main sign that said, "Seventh-day Adventist Church," rather, a sign between the street and the parking lot that said, "Parking for Adventist members only. All others will be towed at their own expense." No joke. I wish I was kidding. I closed my eyes as if I were weary. *Is this really a church*, I muttered to no one in particular, *or is it some secret society?*

After the service, I asked the pastor about the sign. "Oh, I don't like it either," he shook his head and acted embarrassed, "but I don't even notice it anymore. When I first came here, I tried to get them to take it down but they wouldn't budge. I'm afraid if I removed it, they'd slit my throat."

"I'll take it down," I offered. "I'm leaving town tomorrow morning so they can't slit my throat!" He begged me to leave well enough alone.

A year or so later, I went back to that city. The sign was down. A new one reappeared in its place, however, that says, *This parking lot is for the exclusive use of the members of the Seventh-day Adventist congregation.* A little friendlier, perhaps, but still unacceptable. Especially if you notice the second sign nearby with information on how to retrieve your towed automobile from A. C. Towing, Inc.

Unchurched people will not attend a church that is less attractive than their own homes. They will drive up to a neighborhood that is nicer than their own, but they won't drive down to a neighborhood that is uncared for. If the yard around the church is neglected, if the paint is peeling, if the church sign hasn't been updated since the '70s, people will stay away in droves.

I admit that a poor facility seems like a lame cause for a church to plateau. But it happens all the time. It's a major reason why churches can do everything else right and still not grow. So analyze your church. Make sure your building, inside and out, is as attractive as the homes of those you're trying to reach. Count the off-street parking spaces and the seats inside. If your facility stands in the way, fix it or relocate. Because every church stops growing when the price gets too high.

18   Among the majority population, "capacity" means that 80% of the seats are full.

19   Lyle Schaller, *What Have We Learned?*, p. 131.

20   In 1942, 64% of employed Americans walked, rode a bike or rode public transportation to work. In 1998, the numbers were 14%.

21   Statistics apply to majority-population churches in urban and suburban areas.

22   Ellen White, *Christian Service*, p. 228.

HABIT

3

RELATIONSHIPS

*W*e *are all angels with only one wing; we can*
only fly while embracing each other.

—Luciano De Crescenzo

I recently visited the hometown of former Soviet premier Josef Stalin. He was born and raised in a town called Gori in the old Soviet Republic of Georgia. (Gori. Stalin. The two names seem to fit together well, don't they?) That wasn't even his real name. He changed his name to Stalin because the name means "Man of Steel" and he aspired to be a tough guy. When you know he was responsible for the annihilation of up to 65 million of his own people, you walk through the house where he was born and follow the guide through the museum feeling sick to your stomach.

"He was a good man," my taxi driver alleged, as if describing Mother Teresa.

"What was good about him?" I couldn't believe what I just heard.

The driver tried hard to think of something good to say. Stalin is the only well-known person to come from Gori, so many of the locals pretend his atrocities never happened and they all but make him a god. "At least there was order when Stalin was in charge," he finally said.

Stalin had a friend, Nikolai Bukaron, who was one of his advisors. One day, Stalin decided that, for the good of the dictatorship, Bukaron had to go. Stalin called him into his office, pulled out a pistol, said something like, "Sorry, Nikolai, nothing personal." *Boom*! He blew his brains out.

In the church, *everything* is personal. When relationships are healthy, the church is poised to grow. When members fight like scorpions locked in a bottle, the church is as good as dead.

Imagine two churches in town. Both of them believe and teach the same doctrines. One of them is filled with joy, people care for each another, they know they are loved, the church is growing. The other church is harsh. People are divided, unaccepting, critical. Year after year, attendance declines. What makes the difference? Healthy relationships.

Mark Twain, the master of tongue-in-cheek humor, once said that after spending time with good people, he could understand why Jesus preferred to spend His time with sinners.

Everyone loves the *Simpsons*, (well, almost everyone). Their next-door neighbors, Ned and Maude Flanders, are church-going Christians. In one episode, Maude goes away for the weekend. When she returns, Homer wants to know where she has been. "I was at Bible camp," Maude explains. "I was learning how to be more judgmental."

Where is that Bible camp? And why do so many Adventists attend it?

The most Christianized nation in Africa is Rwanda. Ninety-five percent of Rwandans claim to be Christians. Yet what happened there not all that long ago? Millions were slaughtered by fellow Christians. Even many of the clergy participated in murderous rampages.

Leonard Sweet asks a reasonable question: "Why are we more prone to send this post-modern culture hate-mail than love letters? Why can't we teach this culture the best definition of God that has ever been written?"[23] What is that definition? "God is love. Whoever does not love does not know God, for God is love."[24] Paul weighs in and makes it clear when he says, "If I speak in the tongues of men and of angels but have not love, I am only a resounding gong or a clanging cymbal."[25]

When I pastored, I told my members that the fastest way to get a visit from me was to offend someone who is seeking Christ. "I will be at your house before you get there," I threatened, "because it's not going to happen twice." I said it with a smile on my face, but they knew I meant it.

"In this church," I continued, "we have what we call a millstone ministry. In the back room is a stack of millstones—and here's how it works. You offend someone who comes here seeking Christ. We drape one of the stones around your neck and toss you into the sea." They laughed and I joined them, but all of us knew that the idea came from the meek and lowly Jesus.[26]

So here's a multiple-choice quiz, just for fun. Whom did Jesus censure?
- (a) Thieves and prostitutes
- (b) People who ate cheese
- (c) Those who were judgmental and unaccepting.

"Do not judge, and you will not be judged," Jesus taught. "Do not condemn, and you will not be condemned. Forgive and you will be forgiven."[27]

Smokers Welcome Here!

My dad was a pastor. One day he announced to his flock, "I love to smell smoke in church!" Some of the leaders announced they were calling the conference. My dad never handed out cigarettes in church, but here's what he meant: If someone is struggling with that habit—or any habit for that matter—where do they need to be on Sabbath morning? In church. You may be cautious about making them an elder, but they are certainly welcome to attend, and they have every right to expect unconditional love and acceptance as they grow.

I was conducting a reaping series in Ohio. Denise was a Baptist who attended every night. When we covered the Sabbath truth, I invited her to church. She made me an offer. "I'll come on Sabbath if you'll go with me on Sunday." We shook hands and had a deal.

Her pastor was starting a new series on the life of Jesus. His sermon was excellent. Members responded with an occasional *Amen*. I nearly forgot where I was and expelled an *Amen* myself. Directly in front of me, an older lady pivoted 180 degrees, puckered up her face, looked me right in the eye and demanded, "Will you *please* be quiet!" Denise was mortified. I thought it was funny. *So they have people like that, too!* I thought to myself.

Ten minutes later, I tried an *Amen* again. The same lady repeated her previous outburst with even more gusto. Once again, Denise almost disappeared under the pew.

The next Sunday morning, our phone rang. It was early and we were still in bed. My wife covered the receiver and whispered, "It's the Baptist pastor." I cleared my throat and said "Hello."

"I understand you visited our church last Sunday," he got right to the point.

"Yes, I did. And I very much enjoyed it. The service was a blessing. Your message was tremendous." In fact, I had sent him a copy of *The Desire of Ages* that week to help him in his sermon prep.

He ignored my compliments. "I understand that someone offended you during the sermon and I'd like to hear what happened."

"Oh, Pastor, it was nothing. Really. We have people like that, too, and I honestly was not offended."

"Please listen," he was totally focused. "The lady who confronted you has found a way to offend every guest who has ever visited our church. We've tried to help her. We've prayed with her. We've cried with her. We've done everything we know how to do. We told her a few weeks ago that if it happens again, we would remove her from church membership. So I need to know what happened."

I gulped and meekly told the story. Then I wanted to leap out of bed and go to church to see what would happen! Denise told me that night at our meeting. During the morning worship service, the pastor got up and explained to the congregation what had happened last week and the history of it all. He started the process of removing her from church membership but burst into tears. One of the lay leaders took the stage and finished the process of removing this saint from membership of the church.

There may be better venues in which to remove someone from membership. But I still admire the courage of a church that says to its members, "We will be a loving church where those who are different from us, whether socially or spiritually, can be accepted and grow. If you're with us, praise God. If you're against us, you'll have to go somewhere else."

It's tempting to mix up two Bible texts. The first says, "Encourage one another as you see the Day approaching."[28] The other says, "Examine yourself to see if you're in the faith."[29] All too many Christians succumb to the temptation to encourage themselves and to examine one another. God has

THE 7 HABITS OF HIGHLY INEFFECTIVE CHURCHES

not given you—or anyone else—the job of being conscience for someone else. He has told us to encourage each other. So if someone is not living exactly like you think they should or they're not growing spiritually at the pace you recommend, clench your teeth and count to ten. Unless, of course, you're going to put your arm around them and say something like, "You may be going through some things that I don't understand. Whatever it is, I want you to know that I love you and I'll do anything I can to help you."

It is the responsibility of the pastor and lay leaders to create and protect the culture of healthy relationships. Solomon's wisdom is sobering: "A brother offended is harder to win than a strong city."[30]

A cartoon in the Wall Street Journal shows a man who calls home and gets the answering machine. His wife's voice says, "To find out what's for dinner, press 1. To apologize for something you said, press 2. To say 'I love you,' press 3." People in the world are waiting for someone to press 3. Which is precisely why Jesus said, "They will know you are my disciples if you have love for one another."[31]

Another cartoon shows a nurse wheeling her patient down the hall on his bed. Her less-than cheerful words are recorded at the bottom of the scene: "We're moving you from Intensive Care to Indifferent Care."

Confronting the Prophetess

A self-proclaimed prophetess attended a church where I pastored. She was an unhappy person who was in a permanent sensitivity coma. Occasionally, she felt led to share her visions and her counsel. One Sabbath she got really bold while one of my elders was speaking. I was present, but was seated in the audience. Dear Sister Clairvoyant stood to her feet and began to announce the sins of the man who was preaching. Then she recited a list of my sins, most of which I had never thought about doing. The elder handled it appropriately; he just let her wind down then continued with his message.

Afterwards, I was on the warpath. We had guests in church and this lady had just created an obnoxious scene. I pulled her aside privately and told her that what she had done was never to happen again.

"When I have a message from God, I will speak it," she was as stubborn as she was foolish.

"You're free to speak any message you like," I responded, "as long as it's in private."

"If I have a message from God, I will speak it however I choose."

"If you do, it will be the last time you ever set foot in this church." I felt like an umpire sparring with a manager.

"How will you enforce that?" She wanted her bases covered.

"Police." The word rolled off my tongue with unexpected ease.

"You wouldn't do that, would you?"

"That is exactly what I will do. And don't test me in this matter."

She never had any more messages, in public or in private. I don't like confrontation. Just like everyone else, I want everyone to like me. But the time comes when a leader says, "You can't do that around here. Sheep are welcome here, but wolves dressed up like sheep are not."

True or false? Jesus said, "Blessed are the peacekeepers." When a church allows dysfunctional people to dismantle the harmony in the church, they must think the answer is *True*. Actually, that's not what He said. His precise words were, "Blessed are the peacemakers."

What is the difference? A peacekeeper often ignores conflict. He or she pretends it isn't happening or hopes it will go away. Bad apples never get fresh. They only pollute the rest of the box. Peacemaking involves action. It means telling the saint that if she offends another guest, she will lose her membership. It's telling a "prophetess" that her clairvoyance is not welcome here. As I said before, the pastor and lay leaders must do whatever it takes to create and protect the culture of healthy relationships.

A Less-than-Warm Welcome to Church

During my late teenage years, I didn't attend church. To describe me as rebellious would be an understatement. One Sabbath, my girlfriend was in the mood to go to church and persuaded me to join her. We arrived at a church not so far from the one where my dad was the pastor. Surprisingly, I sort of dressed up for the occasion except I didn't wear a tie. Julie wore an attractive pantsuit.

A lady met us at the door. She was the greeter and—believe me—she greeted us with zeal. "I know who your father is, young man," she scowled. "And he would be embarrassed that you went to church without wearing a necktie." I was insulted and made a snide comment about the muumuu she was wearing, but she ignored me and continued her tirade. "And as for you, young lady," she spit in Julie's direction, "you ought to know better than to come to church without wearing a dress. You're not welcome here until you dress properly." Quite a welcome to church, huh?

I know what we should have done. We should have smiled, said *Happy Sabbath*, and walked on in. But neither of us were Christians at that time, so we made some comments consistent with that—and we left. As we climbed in our car to drive away, the dear greeter shouted across the parking lot, "And I'm going to come to your house and tell your father what you did!" *Big deal*, I said to myself. *Come on over!*

A few days later, my dad told me she had called and that she and her husband were indeed coming to our house to talk with my parents about my great crime of going to church without wearing a tie. "Do you want to be in on the meeting?" my dad asked. "Absolutely!" I decided. So there we were in our living room: my dad, my mom, dear Mrs. Saint, her husband, and me.

"Can you believe that your son went to church on Sabbath without wearing a necktie?" the Pharisee began. She droned on and on and lectured my parents about parenting, Sabbath-keeping and compromise. I remember two things from that evening. First, the sadness in my parents' eyes as they tried to comprehend the greeter's bitter spirit. Second, what my father finally said. "Sister, I want you to know that I'm proud of my son for going to church, regardless of how he was dressed, and I'm disappointed that you didn't make him feel welcome."

What would Jesus say? Time for the millstone?

Paul prayed that the church would be "rooted and grounded in love." As Paul's prayer unfolds, it becomes obvious that the love of Christ is more important than information—it "surpasses knowledge." Information is not unimportant, but above all else, the Ephesian Christians were to know and demonstrate the revolutionary love of Christ so that they would "be filled with all the fullness of God."[32]

It's impossible to exaggerate how foundational this is. "If we were more tenderhearted, loving and kind," Ellen White reminds us, "there would be one hundred conversions to the truth where now there is only one."[33] A friend of mine says it this way: "You have to be winsome if you plan to win some."[34]

A Modern Prodigal Son

Wayne was a Sabbath School teacher in a church where I pastored. One day the police came to his house and took him to jail. Everyone was shocked to learn that Wayne and a buddy had been burglarizing homes in several nearby counties. He ended up with a sentence of several years.

I went to visit Wayne in jail. At first, I found it hard to communicate. I couldn't tell if he was embarrassed, bitter or rebellious, but he was definitely distant. As the months rolled by, however, his heart softened. He faced up to what he had done and felt the weight of shame. He asked for God's forgiveness and longed for a chance to make things right.

It was a Friday when Wayne was released. I hoped so much that he would have the guts to come to church the following day. I had to preach in my rural church at 9:30 so I hurried through my sermon and dashed to my larger church.

As I hurried in the door, one of my elders grabbed me by the arm. "Wayne's here!" he discharged the words from an angry face.

"I heard he was released yesterday," I responded. "I'm glad he's back!"

"Well I'm not," he said. "Wayne embarrassed the church and now everyone is oo-ing and awh-ing over him and I think it's disgusting!"

I was almost late getting up on the stage so I didn't have time to respond. "We'll talk later." I hoped he would calm down.

A quarter minute later, a deacon stopped me cold. "Did you hear about 'theify boy?'" he asked cynically.

"What do you mean?" I asked. I was afraid I knew but wanted to make him say it.

"Wayne! He's in church!" his harsh voice hit me like an anvil.

"I'm glad he's here!" I tried to defend him.

"You're glad he's here? As far as I'm concerned, they should've kept him in jail and thrown the key away. I don't want *my* kids around him." He was ready to tie the heretic to the rack or to the stake—take your pick.

I knew what I had to do. When the sermon time came, I set aside my notes and preached on Luke 15, the story of the prodigal son. "This is not just an old story from a dusty book," I said, praying that God would help me apply a timeless lesson to our situation and our time. "This story happened in this town. And it's not over yet because we get to decide how the story ends." And then I took a risk.

"Wayne, would you please come to the front?" Wayne was stunned, but eventually he made his way into the aisle and shuffled to the stage. I wrapped my arm around him and tried to keep my composure. "Many of you know about the events of Wayne's life over the past few years. He made some foolish decisions, hurt his family, and squandered much of his inheritance. It wasn't long till he found himself in a far country living in a place where he was embarrassed to be.

"One day, while in that far country, Wayne came to his senses. His spirit was broken and he said to himself, *I wonder if I can go back. I wonder if anyone still loves me. I wonder if they will forgive me. Maybe I could just return as a servant because I sure don't deserve to be there.* So he found the courage to come back to this church. And I want everyone here to know that *this* church welcomes Wayne back. We are going to wrap the robe of acceptance around him; we are going to kill the fat calf; we're putting a ring on his finger. *This* church is going to celebrate because that which was lost is found!"

The audience broke into a long applause as tears drenched Wayne's face.

Here is a question worth pondering: *If Jesus would not throw the first stone, why should you?* It's all-too easy to crave the grace of God for yourself while withholding it from someone else. One of the highest duties of church leaders is to create the climate of unconditional love in the church—to make it plain that God loves every sinner *while they are yet sinners.* Whether or not we treat people as Jesus did is not optional. "If we love one another," John reminds us, "God abides in us."[35]

Ask these questions about your church.
- Do we truly want lost people here?
- Are they safe here?
- Do we truly love and respect one another?
- Are we safe here?

As followers of Jesus, we are to live by faith, but be known by our love. Make sure the other habits are in place, create and tenaciously protect the culture of healthy relationships, and watch your conversions soar.

And by the way, every church stops growing when the price gets too high.

23   Leonard Sweet, *Soul Tsunami,* p. 425.

24   I John 4:8.

25   I Corinthians 13:1, NIV.

26   See Luke 17:2.

27   Luke 6:36, 37.

28   Hebrews 13:5.

29   I Corinthians 13:5.

30   Proverbs 18:19, NKJV.

31   John 13:35.

32   See Ephesians 3:17-19.

33   Ellen White, *Testimonies,* Vol. 9, p. 189.

34   Thanks to Mel Waters.

35   I John 4:12.

H A B I T

4

EVANGELISM

The idea that you could become a mature Christian and not have a heart that is broken for those who are lost is inconceivable.

—Erwin Raphael McManus

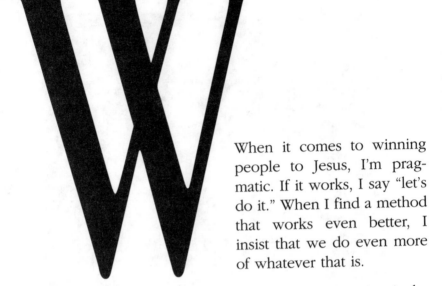

When it comes to winning people to Jesus, I'm pragmatic. If it works, I say "let's do it." When I find a method that works even better, I insist that we do even more of whatever that is.

One of the primary reasons that churches stop growing is the way they do (or don't do) evangelism. It's common for members to verbalize their love for Jesus, but their witness consists of dropping their offering in the plate so that someone more qualified can communicate the good news. Church leaders are hopeful, but they wonder out loud if anyone really knows how to reach the lost. Like a VCR on pause, the whole church seems to hesitate as if waiting for something new to try.

This chapter is divided into four parts:
- (a) why some evangelistic methods that work in one country don't work in another,
- (b) how our current methods inadvertently exclude the majority of people who need Christ,
- (c) the four paradigm shifts that will drastically broaden our understanding of evangelism,
- (d) how every follower of Christ can participate in evangelism that really works—and have a blast doing it.

Dennis Prager is a talk show host in Southern California. Every year, he conducts a survey among high-school seniors. He's been doing it for 15 years. Every year he asks the same question, and every year he receives the same response. Here's the question: *If both were drowning, which would you save first, your dog or a stranger?*

How do you think the young people answered? One-third of the high-school seniors said they would save their dog. One-third said they would save the stranger. And one-third said the question was too difficult to answer.

I don't know how I would have answered the question when I was a high-school senior, but I know how I would answer it now. I would save the stranger. Part of the reason is because of my dog. I love McKenna, but there have been times when I was ready to wring her neck. Like the time we left her in the house while we were gone and she dragged the sofa out into the middle of the room with her teeth and ripped the fabric to shreds! So I would definitely save the stranger.

And I have some advice for you. If you're going to drown, be sure to wait until there are at least three high school seniors nearby because two of them won't do you any good.

Prager followed up with a question just for the two out of three who did not choose the stranger: "Why on earth wouldn't you save the person?" Here's what they said: "I know my dog; I don't know the stranger. I love my dog; I don't love the stranger. I have feelings for my dog; I don't have feelings for the stranger."

Do you love the stranger? Do you have feelings for someone whom you don't even know their name? Do you care—deeply and passionately—about where someone will spend eternity even if you don't know who they are?

Jesus looked at the crowds and His heart was broken. "When He saw the multitudes, He was moved with compassion for them, because they were weary and scattered, like sheep having no shepherd."[36] One of the primary reasons churches stop growing is that members care so little about what broke Jesus' heart. And even when they do care, they are often perplexed about how to reach people in a secular society with the gospel.

You Actually Live in Athens

You may think you live in North America, but you actually live in Athens. Spiritually, the United States and Canada (as well as the other Western countries) are amazingly similar to the Athens of Paul's day. People are cynical, confused, and resistant to the truth.

In Acts 17, Paul preached in three cities—Thessalonica, Berea and Athens. Afterward, when he had time to reflect, Paul must have thought, *Wow. Those places weren't anything alike. It's like I visited three different planets!*

Thessalonica: Conversions, but stiff persecution

It was Sabbath and Paul entered the synagogue. His name wasn't in the bulletin, but he knew he would preach. Sure enough, it wasn't long till the Spirit said *Now!* and Paul stood to his feet. In a conscious act of audacity, he proclaimed that Jesus was the Christ. Conversions occurred left and right, especially among the Greeks. So far, so good.

"But the hard-line Jews became furious over the conversions. Mad with jealousy, they rounded up a bunch of brawlers off the streets and soon had an ugly mob terrorizing the city as they hunted down Paul and Silas."[37] To save their lives, the believers whisked the evangelists out of town under the dim glow of suffocated stars.

Berea: Lots of conversions, no internal persecution

The next town was different. It was an easy place to work. Paul preached, people pondered, and plenty were persuaded. The journalist Luke reports that "these were more noble than those in Thessalonica, in that they received the word with all readiness of mind, and searched the Scriptures daily."[38]

Even more exciting, it was apparently the Jews who led the way in receiving the gospel. From the poor to the rich, the peasant to the prominent, the Bereans absorbed the truth like quicksand. Later, persecution arrived from Thessalonica, but none from Berea itself. *If every town were like Berea,* Paul mused, *these missionary trips would be a cinch.*

Athens: Few conversions

Then there was Athens—a virtual junkyard of idols. "It is plain to see that you Athenians take your religion very seriously,"[39] Paul announced when he finally got their ear. He spoke the truth. Athens was indeed very religious. Worshippers chose their god of the month from an idol-rich menu. Their fascination with theories revealed a frightening mix of intelligence and naiveté. The result? Few received the Messiah.

Paul never planted a church in Athens. If he wrote a letter to the Athenians, we've never seen it. Yet in *Acts of the Apostles,* Ellen White heaps praise on Paul for his efforts and his methods in Athens. She calls his ministry there a "victory for Christianity in the very heart of paganism."[40] Paul wasn't used to this kind of victory, but—hey!—this was Athens!

Our World in the 21st Century

The cities of Acts 17 help us understand our world today. When it comes to spiritual receptivity, interest varies wildly from place to place but generally corresponds to one of these three cities.

Thessalonica: Restricted Nations

Some countries of the world are like Thessalonica. We preach the gospel and people are converted, but thunderous persecution results. All of these countries are dominated by either Islamic or communist regimes where Adventists and other Christians are generally mystified as to how to advance the kingdom.

The Voice of the Martyrs (VOM)[41] lists 42 countries as "restricted nations." By definition, these are places where (a) Christians are kept from obtaining Bibles or other Christian literature by government policy or practice, and (b) the local governments sanction Christians being harassed, imprisoned, deprived of their possessions and liberties or even killed because of their faith in Jesus Christ.[42] VOM estimates that 165,000 Christians were martyred for their faith in the year 2002 in restricted countries such as China, Sudan, North Korea and Tunisia.[43]

Paul and Silas were able to escape from Thessalonica; they might find it more difficult to escape from a restricted nation today.

Berea: Open Nations

Other countries are like Berea. It's fun to evangelize in Berea! We bring a team of workers and thousands are converted. The laws of the land support our work. The people are ravenous for Bibles and for the truth. Examples include Papua New Guinea, parts of Africa, India, much of Central America.

Consider Pastor Dave, a friend who recently conducted a reaping series in a "Berean" country. He returned to America with his face glowing like Moses' on Sinai. Stories spilled out of him like chemicals from a crop duster. His photos were astonishing; he insisted I see every one. From where he stood on the platform to preach each evening, it was impossible to see where the crowds of people ended. On the final Sabbath, multiplied hundreds of brand-new Christians followed Jesus in baptism. I praised God with him at the mighty moving of the Spirit.

Evangelism in Berea is thrilling. It gives us hope. It assures us that God is still blessing the Church.

Athens: First World Nations

Pastor Dave returned to his own hometown and preached a reaping series. Same preacher, same sermons, same computer, same Holy Spirit. He baptized eleven. What is the difference? He lives in "Athens."[44]

The United States is Athens. Canada is Athens. Australia, New Zealand and most of Europe are Athens. Spiritual receptivity is different here, especially among the majority population, and we shouldn't be surprised. Didn't Jesus warn that some cities would be tough? "Just expect it," He said. "When you find a city where they'll listen, preach! When they won't, shake the dust off your feet and move on."[45]

Paul had that option so that's what he did. It was the right thing to do. There were only a few of them so he eagerly followed Jesus' advice and sought out the next Berea. Could Paul have evangelized Athens? Certainly. If Paul's conference president had said, "Paul, stay in Athens and don't leave until you've planted a church!" without a doubt, he could have done it. Progress would have been slow, but he would have planted a church.

We are stuck in Athens. The Gospel Commission demands that we minister here. Once every year or two some are able to slip away for an evangelistic blitzkrieg in Berea, but our primary assignment is to reach the lost right where we live.

Here are our options. First, we can ignore the people of Athens and conclude that they don't care about God. We can throw up our hands in pretended concern and say, "They know where our churches are. If they were interested, they would come." Or, instead, we can resolve, "We are not afraid of Athens. No way! Our mission is clear: To take the message of Jesus smack dab into the heart of the toughest places on earth. We will stare this challenge in the face and, under the Holy Spirit, we will not shrink back. In fact, with God, we will prevail."

Some Basic Assumptions
Let's build on these assumptions:

- Soul winning is in the Adventist DNA. Clearly, our approach is less effective than in years gone by, but we still truly care. If we knew what to do, we would do it.
- The people of Athens are spiritually polarized. While many drift off into postmodernism or other religions, thousands of others from all ages and backgrounds are joining churches. In either case, they are truly seeking God.
- What works in Berea may or may not work in Athens. (Just ask Paul.)
- What used to work in Athens in a previous era is only relevant if it's still effective today.
- When the church radically lives the gospel and communicates the message in ways appropriate with the times, we will experience a vigorous revival.[46]

▪ "Too-narrow" Evangelism

Our current evangelistic methods are OK, but they're too narrow. When our local church announces that it is planning to do "evangelism," we all know what to expect; a very specific picture comes to mind. Other Christians don't use the word "evangelism" the way we do, but here's what we envision.

- We will host an event that happens 4 nights a week for 5 weeks (or so).
- A professional will make the presentations, sometimes in person, sometimes from a distant city via satellite.[47]
- The event will interrupt the life of the church. When it's over, we'll get back to doing church as usual.
- We will spend a lot of money advertising to people whom we've never met.
- We will measure success by the number of baptisms.
- It will appeal to an ever-shrinking minority in our community.

Two issues contribute to the shrinking. First is the simple issue of time. Suppose you receive a flyer in the mail inviting you to attend a seminar on your favorite topic (trekking in Nepal? remodeling your house?). Then you notice that it meets 4 nights a week for 5 weeks. Could you attend? Probably not.

Thirty years ago, Americans had much more free time. Today, when we offer a series of meetings that convenes 20+ times in 5 weeks, we exclude most people while attracting primarily the retired, unemployed and socially unique. They are indeed unique simply because it's not normal in today's fast-paced life to have that kind of time. There are exceptions, but they are rare. Of course retired, unemployed and socially unique people matter to God, but unless our methods of evangelism are broader, we will win fewer and fewer of the majority in each community.

The second issue has to do with curiosity about the Bible. According to one study, 4% of Americans say they would be interested in attending a seminar to learn more about the Bible and prophecy.[48] Those numbers were no doubt dramatically different three or four decades ago.

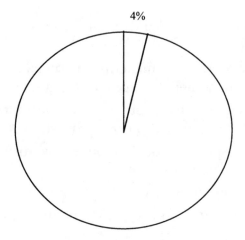

4%

If we plot the 4% on a pie chart, it looks something like this. As time goes along, we find ourselves having to spend more and more money to attract a crowd from this ever-narrowing slice of the population. And what about the other 96%? Whether consciously or not, they are all seeking for God. How will we reach them?

Consider the Evangelism Scale.[49]

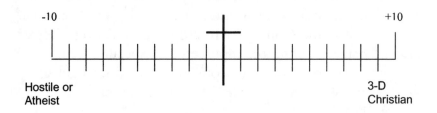

Someone who, spiritually, is a long way from God is a minus ten. The steps toward the cross indicate warming up toward Christianity until, at the cross, the person chooses to be a Christ-follower. The steps east of the cross denote spiritual growth with the eventual goal of becoming a definitely devoted disciple or what I call a 3-D Christian.

Reflect on the 4% who say they would be interested in attending a seminar to learn more about the Bible and prophecy. What is true about them in relationship to the evangelism scale? Most of them believe in absolute truth[50] and would like to learn more about the Bible. If we were to plot them on the scale, they would be very close to the cross, at minus one or two. When our only evangelism is the semi-often event, we appeal to people close to the cross and unwittingly exclude the rest. Since they stay away from our meetings, we make the tragic assumption that they don't care about God.

Average Americans—who are somewhere in the neighborhood of minus 6 on the scale—do indeed care about God. Down deep in their heart of hearts, they know there is a final answer. Sure they're confused about the Bible. Ask them what word comes to mind when they think of church and their answer will fall somewhere between "Boring" and "Leave me alone." But in their own way, they are seeking. And we can reach many of them with the gospel.

Paradigm Shifts

If we're ready to broaden our definition of evangelism, we have to start with four paradigm shifts.

1. The goal of the Gospel Commission is to make disciples.

For years, we have been confused about the Gospel Commission. We thought Jesus said, "Go ye therefore and baptize" when He actually said, "Go and make disciples." So the evangelist knows exactly what he wants: baptisms. The conference president demands to know, "How many did you baptize?"

Jesus did not say, "Go into all the world and get people to say a salvation prayer." He never said, "Repeat after me." He said, "Follow me." As long as people stop certain behaviors and start others, as long as they stop believing wrong things about God and start believing the truth, we baptize them and send their names on to the conference. "Job well done!" we say to ourselves.

But as rare as penguins in Peoria are churches with a discipleship track to help the new member actually become a definitely devoted disciple. And what exactly is a disciple? One who has the character and priorities of Jesus. Not just the character of Jesus (which we often define with a list of wrong behaviors that must be avoided), but also the priorities of Jesus. How Jesus spent His time. What and whom He valued. What was most important. "The one who believes in me," Jesus says, "will also do the works that I do and, in fact, will do greater works than these."[51] The implications of these words are indeed profound.

Traditional evangelism starts with people who are already close to the cross. Through a 4-5 week marathon of meetings, the Holy Spirit moves them a notch or two to the point of decision which, on the evangelism scale, is represented by the cross. With their clothes still wet from their baptism, the evangelist tows his trailer to the next town; his work is done.

And so is that of the church. Which explains the high apostasy rate among persons baptized through a series of meetings. Which also explains, for example, why we have the same divorce rate in the Adventist church as in the general population. Nearly every other dysfunction of society is common in the church as well, because we thought the goal was to baptize when actually it is to create definitely devoted disciples.

2. Evangelism is not an event; it is a process.
Every farmer knows that you reap in a different season than you sow. Unfortunately, few church leaders have figured that out yet and even fewer plan their evangelism accordingly.

Winning people to Jesus has always been a process. In 1 Corinthians, Paul says, "I planted, Apollos watered, and God gave the increase."[52] Paul never expected to lead every person he met to Christ. Sure, whenever he met someone, he'd hope he could persuade them, but reality all-too-often trumps wishful thinking. "I'll do my part," he says, "then trust that God will bring Apollos along to water the seed. And I'm confident that God can be counted on to give the increase."

Jesus told the woman at the well, "My food is to do the will of Him who sent me and to finish His work. Do you not say four months more and then the harvest?[53] I tell you, open your eyes and look at the fields. They are ripe for harvest."

I have always read this as motivation to get out and do evangelism because the harvest fields are ready. One could certainly argue that point with some authority. But notice what Jesus says next: "Thus the saying, one sows and another reaps is true. I sent you to reap what you have not worked for. Others have done the hard work and have reaped the benefits of their labor."[54]

The meaning of Jesus' words is clear. The hard work of sowing is distinct from the relative ease of reaping. If someone has been doing the work of sowing, the fields will be ripe for harvest. If no one has been sowing, the fields cannot possibly be ripe for harvest.

When evangelism becomes more than just an event, thousands will find salvation. But let's be honest. We're addicted to the quick fix. We want instant results. The evangelist is taught to think, *Who needs Apollos? If I don't get the decision now, they may never make it.*

So we don't mind spending a lot of money to get a crowd of strangers in the church, and we'll cover everything they need to know in a handful of weeks, so we can fast-track the result.

The event we call evangelism has pushed aside the process like an untended weed in the grass. Anything else the church does is pooh-poohed as not really evangelism. Which brings us to our third paradigm shift.

3. We have to redefine some terms.
Evangelism

If the 4-5 week event is our definition of evangelism, what does that say about everything else the church does? It isn't evangelism. And since it isn't, we don't really try. We shouldn't be too surprised when, apart from the evangelistic series, baptisms are an infrequent occurrence.

Everything a church does can be and should be evangelism. Accordingly, it is urgent that we change our vocabulary. We have to force ourselves to stop calling the 4-5 week event "evangelism." My tongue no longer permits me to use the word so narrowly. Neither did Ellen White's. "Preaching," she wrote, "is a small part of the work to be done for the salvation of souls."[55]

The 4-5 week event is not evangelism. It is a part of evangelism—a vital part when done as one element in the process—but by itself, it is not evangelism.

Instead, let's call it *reaping*, or the *harvest event*. Rewind to the '50s, and you'll find that what we currently call evangelism used to, in fact, be reaping. Here's a nugget of history.

One of our most respected evangelists was Fordyce Detamore; he preached the Three Angel's message with vein-popping passion. He and his family moved into a city, settled in for half-a-year or longer, and preached as often as six nights a week.[56]

One day it dawned on him that if he spent so long in one place, he wouldn't live long enough to evangelize all the cities that needed him. To reflect the urgency of the task, Detamore

THE 7 HABITS OF HIGHLY INEFFECTIVE CHURCHES

invented what he called the "short crusade" or the "lightning crusade," a condensed, to-the-point series of meetings that presented the entire Adventist message in six weeks. The intent of such a series was clearly reaping. If a person had no contact with the church before the meetings started, he would only approve that person for baptism if they participated in an intense and accelerated baptismal class.[57]

What have we done today? Taken the six week reaping series, compressed it down to five, four or even three weeks. And since we almost never have contact with non-Adventists before the series begins, we advertise to total strangers who don't even know we are Adventists, then turn the extra-short series into the entire process of evangelism. We urge people to hurry and get baptized, then when they leave, we scratch our heads and lament that the information transfer was not enough to ground them in the church.

Evangelist
The second term we must redefine is "Evangelist." If the person who tows his trailer into town—or speaks from a distant city via satellite—is the evangelist, what does that say about rest of us? We aren't. And since we aren't, it seems perfectly logical that we shouldn't worry too much about doing it. We'll just leave the job to the pro.

We have to redefine the word. If the 4-5 week event is called Reaping, what should we call the person who leads the reaping? The obvious answer is "Reaper." However, some have succumbed to the temptation to add the word "Grim" before "Reaper" so that won't do. We have instead chosen to call this person the "Reaping Specialist."

Really, that's what they are. They're outstanding at what they do. But as long as we call them the evangelist, we will continue to send the message that the task of winning people to Jesus is up to them. *We'll keep the church humming along,* we think, *and when we need some baptisms, we'll bring in Mark Finley or Dan Bentzinger.* So we have to change our vocabulary. What we used to call "Evangelism" we now call "Reaping." The guy we used to label "Evangelist" is the "Reaping Specialist." And everyone else in the church—from the eight year old child, to the person who isn't even baptized yet, to the seasoned lay member—becomes an evangelist in a way that matches their spiritual maturity and their spiritual gifts.

Sanctuary

You have to agree with me on the first two redefinitions, but this one is optional; you can agree or disagree. I think we need to redefine the word "Sanctuary." What, literally, does the word mean? The dictionary says: "A place of refuge or asylum. A reserved area in which animals or birds are protected."

When we refer to the room where we worship God as the sanctuary, we aren't really being Biblical. Since the cross, the Bible speaks of two sanctuaries: one is in heaven, the other is the human heart.

Furthermore, we send the wrong message when we call the place where we meet, the sanctuary. A sanctuary is for protection. Do we come apart on Sabbath to protect ourselves from something? From what, the evil world? We go to church not to *protect* ourselves but to *prepare* ourselves to go out into the world and demonstrate God's love. So, as I said, you don't have to agree with me, but I think the church could more easily recapture its passion for mission if we stopped reinforcing the notion that the world is bad, the church is good and we come together to protect ourselves. That way of thinking, in fact, is the root of our problem.

What should we call the place where we meet to worship God? How about the Worship Center? Or as one of my friends suggested, since we call the place where we play the gym-nasium, why not call the place where we worship the God-nasium?[58]

4. The great commission does not say "Come," it says "Go."

The fourth paradigm shift is especially profound. Almost exclusively, we do church as if the gospel commission was given to the lost, telling them to come to our churches. So we create events: health programs, reaping series, Bible study classes—sometimes at major expense—then hope people will come to us.

A popular Christian book title says it well: *Out of the Saltshaker and into the World.*[59] The gospel commission was not given to the lost, telling them to come. It instead was given to us, telling us to go.

Just to be sure, I looked up the word "Go" in the dictionary. It says: "To move or travel. To move away from a place; depart. To function properly, as in: *The car won't go."* The problem, it seems, is that the *believers* won't go.

When I was a kid, my dad pastored several churches. It seemed like every Sabbath afternoon, most of the members were out in the community doing something evangelistic. We took surveys, distributed Bibles, signed people up for studies, or invited them to some church event. If you didn't join the crowd on Sabbath afternoon, the church had a name for you. They called you an inactive member. You could attend church every Sabbath morning, but if you didn't go out into the community to engage in missionary activity, you were considered inactive. I know what you're thinking: *Our lingo has sure changed!* It has. The church used to epitomize the word "Go", but, obviously, no longer does. What happened? For one thing, society has changed. But I think something else happened in North America that pushed us from *Go* to *Come.*

In 1975, a group of young people in Northwest Chicago started a church to reach people who had given up on church. They knocked themselves out to create a safe place where people whom they called "seekers" could investigate the Christian faith. Once they made a commitment, they could join a small group or a ministry team and take their spiritual growth to the next level. It worked like magic. Why?

Willow Creek did the right thing at the right time. They capitalized on a sociological phenomenon whereby Baby Boomers who had drifted away from church started coming back to expose their kids to Christian beliefs. Willow was ready with a seven-step process that started with unchurched people, then moved them a step at a time to become "Fully Devoted Followers." A major part of that process was the Seeker service. *We'll design a special service,* they decided, *specifically for those who may be seeking Christ. It's not a worship service—we'll do that, too—but it's sensitive to where they are spiritually. It's Christianity 101, entry-level stuff, for those who don't know much about God but would like to explore the Christian faith.* Their paradigm was perfect for the last quarter century. *You're returning to church for your kids' sake? Come. You'll be safe here. We'll help you grow.*

Society has changed. The Baby Boomers are no longer bringing their kids to church. For obvious reasons: their kids are grown up. The generation that followed are not bringing their kids to church. Many of us have learned from Willow Creek and have been blessed by their love for God and passion for the lost. But if you do church today on the "Come" paradigm, you will fail. Especially today, the church must "Go". So we stumble onto another word that needs to be redefined.

Seeker

For years, we have used the word "Seeker" to refer to lost people who are beginning to search for God. It's a reasonable definition, but it is based on Come instead of Go. The passing of the wave of Boomer returnees to church means the church must now take the initiative. It must move from being the inviting church to becoming the infiltrating church. It is not enough for the church to be seeker-sensitive. The church *itself* must become the seeker. The ultimate seeker was Jesus Christ who came to seek to save the lost.[60] To be faithful to our mission, to follow in His footsteps, we are today's seekers. Robert Lewis is correct when he says, "We can no longer afford to stand on one side of the chasm and shout to those on the other side. We must connect."[61]

An All-too Typical Church

My office phone rang one morning. On the other end was a friend who pastored two time zones away. "Hey, Ron. Do you have a few minutes?" I always have time for a friend.

"Can you give me some pointers for my church? We're having a hard time breaking our plateau and I'm wondering if you can help."

"I'll try. Tell me about your church."

As he searched for words to describe his church, it occurred to me that I had heard a nearly-identical story a hundred times through the lips of other pastors. "Do you have a pen and some paper?" I asked. "Draw the evangelism scale. You know, horizontal line, cross in the middle, minus 10 on the left, plus 10 on the right."

"Got it!" he said.

"OK, tell me everything your church does, then make a mark either left or right of the cross."

"We have worship service every Sabbath," he started.

"Is that primarily left or right of the cross?"

"Right of the cross." He answered without a heartbeat of hesitation. "Then every Sabbath this summer, we're inviting everyone who attends the morning service to a picnic in the park or some other social deal."

"Left or right of the cross?" I asked again.

"I guess it's right, huh? Because they wouldn't know about it unless they were at church."

"Right on. What else does your church do?"

"We have two small groups that meet on Tuesday nights in members' homes."

"What do they do?" I asked.

"They're studying different books of the Bible."

"Left or right of the cross?" I was beginning to sound redundant, even to myself.

"Right of the cross. And we have another small group on Friday night that studies last-day events. So that's right of the cross, too."

"What else?" I wanted to make sure he didn't leave something out.

"That's all," he conceded. "What do you think?"

"Well, how does your evangelism scale look? Where are the marks?"

"Oh no!" he sputtered. "Everything we're doing is right of the cross. For people who have already committed to be Christians. We're not doing anything for people left of the cross!"

He put his finger on the pulse of the problem. The average North American is somewhere in the vicinity of minus 6 on the evangelism scale. Yet almost everything the church does is right of the cross. Then we're bewildered as to why people don't take the flying leap from minus 6—or wherever they are —to the things we do in our own little world we call church.

We ended the conversation with one of my favorite mantras: "If evangelism is not your top priority, it will not make the top ten."

Where is the Church in Your Town?

If you ask me *Where is the Adventist church in Buffalo?* I will ask you, *What time is it?*

What kind of answer is that?

I was hoping you'd ask. If it's 11:30 on Sabbath morning, I'll tell you the street and the number. If it's 11:30 on Tuesday morning, where is the church in Buffalo? Spread all over the city, going about their work and their school, while living for Christ.

The church is not the building—it's the people. Imagine a church where every person who attends sees himself or herself as a "God-connector." Imagine a church where everyone prays and expects God to use them to nudge someone toward Christ. Imagine a church where every person prioritizes their calendar and uses their spiritual gifts to help someone find salvation through Jesus Christ.

New Definitions

I hope you agree that we need some new definitions. So here goes.

Evangelism: Everything a church does. This includes connecting with people wherever they are and moving them one notch right on the evangelism scale. As part of the process, it includes—but is certainly not limited to—a semi-often reaping series.

Evangelist: One who consistently
- Attends

- Builds one-on-one friendships with those left of the cross
- Participates in church-initiated activities designed for those left of the cross.

We call this "Evangelism by Nudge." As individuals, we build friendships with those left of the cross. As a church, we create venues and opportunities to connect with pre-Christians and pray that God will use our influence to move them a notch at a time toward Christ.

Make Everyone an Evangelist

I was teaching a seminar when a gentleman raised his hand. "Ron, when the dust settles at the end of the world, will anyone really be lost if I don't share my faith?"

"Yes," I answered. "You."

If you're serious about reaching the lost in Athens, you can't rely solely on the professional; everyone must be an evangelist. Or if you prefer a different word than evangelist, how about this: Make everyone a "God-connector"—one who connects others with God.

This is another of those rules that we don't get to vote on. Everyone who decides to be a follower of Jesus is given the ministry of reconciliation—not just those who are in full-time, paid ministry.[62] When you take seriously God's call to connect others to Him, two things happen. First, you experience unprecedented spiritual growth personally—you understand God's heart and you pour out your life to honor Him. Second, the gospel exerts its power and the church prospers.

My audience was a group of college kids and I knew I had to be creative. I once heard a pastor play a word association game so I decided to steal it and pretend I thought of it first.

"Let's play a game," I started. "I'll name a vocation; you create a picture in your mind. Are you ready? Here's the first word: Librarian."

They described a woman with glasses on her nose and a bun on her head. Her index finger bisected her lips in an effort to keep everyone quiet.

"Next word: Fisherman."

They pictured a man standing in a stream wearing waders, clutching a pole in one hand and a net in the other.

"Next word: Sumo wrestler."

"A fat man with a diaper!" a girl yelled out.

"Last word: Evangelist."

The room was quiet. The mental wheels were turning, but it took a while before someone ventured an answer. With a little prodding, they finally described Kenneth Cox or C.D. Brooks.

It was time for the punch line. "When I said the word "Evangelist," how many of you thought of yourselves?" Every hand was limp. "My goal," I announced, "is to change that during the next 45 minutes."

When the session was over, I asked them again, "Now that you understand the broader definition of evangelism, how many of you could see yourself as an evangelist?" Every hand was raised.

What did I tell them? A variety of ways of being an evangelist that fit into four different categories.

Evangelism for the Rest of Us

The list of ways to connect with people and move them one notch right is infinite, but I've organized them into four definable groups.

1. Hang Out with People Who Need Jesus.

George Barna is affectionately known to many as "Bad-news Barna" because his research often uncovers things we wish we didn't know. For example, Barna reports that fewer than 1 out of 10 American Christians ever attempts to build a friendship with a lost person in hopes of someday leading them to Christ. Fewer than 1 out of 10 even *tries*. I suspect that the Adventist ratio is the same.

The longer a person is a Christian, the fewer unchurched friends they tend to have. Without deliberate effort, we find ourselves spending more and more time with the already-convinced and less and less time with people who are lost.

Ask yourself this question: "The last time I invited someone to my house on a Saturday night, whom did I invite?" I'll bet I can answer for you; the responses are always the same. It's easier and more comfortable to hang out with people like ourselves. Spending time with secular people is scary. You never know what they might say. Maybe they'll eat or drink something that you don't consume. What if they use language that you can't bring into church?

It's not wrong to invite other Adventists to our house once in a while. We enjoy the fellowship and we need to have fun together. But what if 2 out of 3 times, the person we invite is a non-believer—someone who will probably not go to heaven unless something changes between now and Jesus' return?

Jesus should be our example. (Remember our definition of a disciple? One who has the character and the priorities of Jesus.) Think about the evangelism scale and ponder this: "Where did Jesus spend most of His time, left or right of the cross?" On Sabbath morning, He was in the synagogue which we could argue is right of the cross. What about the rest of the week? Didn't He spend the overwhelming majority of His time with those on the left of the cross? "Those who are well do not need a physician, but those who are sick. I did not come to call the righteous," He reminds us, "but sinners to repentance."[63]

Adventists have heard a thousand preachers recite *Ministry of Healing*, page 143. "Christ's method alone will bring success in reaching the people." Then without consciously thinking of the evangelism scale, Ellen White adds, "Jesus mingled among men as One who desired their good. He won their confidence, met their needs, then He bade them *Follow Me.*"[64]

We have violated the foundational element of reaching the lost —we don't mingle as Jesus did—and we assume it doesn't matter. *We don't need to,* we reason. *Every year or two we'll do a reaping series and cough up enough money to mail a flyer to thousands of strangers. Once they're on our turf, we'll tell them what they need to know.*

Some of today's saints have even sided with the Pharisees and concluded that being with secular people is wrong! *Let's see,* they reason. *Jesus is our example in most things, but we wouldn't dare emulate Him by actually associating with people who are lost, would we?*

Fifty thousand flyers mailed to total strangers will not finish the work. Project Sow One Billion will convince some of the Sabbath, but not much else. DVD evangelism, satellite dishes, Bible lessons on CD-ROM or the internet will have minimal impact. Your church will not become an unstoppable force until it is normal for every member to do what Jesus did. Christ's method alone will bring success. Not to the exclusion of the other good things, but as the foundation for everything else.

Christ's method alone. Flash it on the screen on Sabbath morning. Print it prominently in the bulletin and in your newsletter. Post it on your website. Hang it on your fridge. Challenge one another to live as Jesus lived. Mingle with the lost as one who desires their good. Make premeditated friendship a soaring, non-negotiable priority in your life and in your schedule.

A pastor friend of mine complained that his members wouldn't help with evangelism. "They're mostly professional people, they have kids at home and they're just too busy," he lamented.

"Do they ever go on a picnic?" I asked him. "Do they ever go to a ball game?"

"Yes," he assured me. "But they don't have time to do evangelism." What he meant, of course, was Bible studies or public meetings.

"What would happen if whenever they went on a picnic or to the ball game, they invited a neighbor to join them?" I started to unravel his concern. "What if each family had a list of 5 or 10 people who are not going to heaven unless something changes? What if they schemed and conspired to mingle with them, doing the things they enjoy doing, all the while praying that their friendship and God's blessing will move their neighbor one notch closer to the cross?

"What if you modeled that for them and told your stories? What if everyone challenged each other to do what Jesus did? What if you had a time on Sabbath and a place in your newsletter where everyone swapped stories and prayed for their friends?

"If a member likes scrap booking, they should ask a neighbor to join them. When their family is going camping, they can invite someone they work with to come along. If they're into ice skating or biking or volleyball, they can enjoy it with someone whose life isn't all together yet. Hang out with people. Mingle."

My pastor friend got it. Hanging out with lost people has moved to the top of his must-do list.

Here are four simple rules for mingling:

(1) Remember that God is already working in their life. Your appearance isn't the first time God has tugged at their heart.

(2) Don't talk until you've listened. Pay attention to their story. Try to recognize exactly how God is already working in their life.

(3) When they ask or when the Holy Spirit says, *Now!*, communicate in a way that connects their story to the story of Jesus.

(4) Whatever else you do, leave them feeling positive about your encounter. Remember that your job is to love them, listen to them, and pray that they will move one notch to the right. By all means, do not pressure them or you may end up moving them a notch or two *away* from the cross.

On an individual basis, as an individual imitator of Christ, make the commitment to hang out with people who need Jesus.

2. Knock on a Stranger's Door.

This one scares some people half to death. They'd rather swallow strychnine than knock on someone's door. But not so fast. This survey is different. Everyone enjoys it whether they're on the outside or inside of the door. And it's certainly a left-of-cross activity.

Here are the questions:

(1) When you think of church, what word comes to mind?

(2) If you could ask God any question, what would you ask?

(3) Is there anything in life you wouldn't give up, no matter what?

(4) I'm part of a church that wants to be relevant in this community. What advice do you have for me?

When the survey is finished, ask almost as an afterthought, "By the way, do you have someone you consider to be your pastor?" If they say "Yes," say, "That's great. Would it be OK if I pray for your pastor?" If they don't have a pastor, hand them a business card and say, "Now you do. I'd love to be your pastor. If you ever need anything, please feel free to call on me." (If you're not a pastor, adapt your answer accordingly and either give them your pastor's card or one of your own.)

Be clear on the purpose of the survey. First, you do it to learn about your community, about how people view church and God. You'll likely find that you are blessed more than those whom you contact. Second, you pray that God will put you in touch with someone you can bless. Not someone you can convince to join your church, but someone you can bless. There is a difference. (Jesus mingled among men as One who desired their good.) Joining your church is—best case scenario—in their future, but your primary motivation is to be a blessing.

Normally, you're done in a couple of minutes. Sometimes, the person opens up and asks for your help or your prayers. Like the big, tough guy in Everett, Washington who answered Question Two like this: "I would ask God, why am I dying of cancer?" Be sensitive both to the person at the door and to the Holy Spirit. Be ready to serve however you can.

I was speaking to pastors in Romania and gave them an assignment. "Find 10 strangers," I instructed them, "and ask them the four survey questions." We had a drawing for those who completed the task. The next morning, several came up and reported on the exciting experiences they had. One pastor was so wound up, he could hardly wait his turn. He reported the following story.

A lady was at a bus stop and appeared to be crying. She looked approachable so he asked if she would answer 4 questions, "no strings attached." She agreed. Question 1: "When you think of church, what word comes to mind?" Her answer: "My childhood." Question 2: "If you could ask God any question, what would you ask?" Her answer: "I would ask God, Where is my little dog?" She explained that her dog had been missing for several days. She had looked everywhere. It was her only friend and she was heartbroken. The pastor asked if they could pray about it, and right there at the bus stop, he prayed. When the prayer was over, he asked Question 3: "Is there anything in life you wouldn't give up, no matter what?" Her answer: "My little dog." Question 4: "I'm a pastor. What advice do you have for me?" Her answer: "Please help me find my little dog!"

The pastor decided he should try. When the bus arrived to take her home, he got on with her. They got off at the stop near her apartment building and began walking toward her home. They rounded the last corner and right in front of them was her little dog, running straight for her. It leaped into her arms. She wept and thanked the pastor for helping her, amazed that God cared enough to reunite her with her dog! One moment she was friendless, the next she was eager to learn more about the God who cares. (Now there is a dog worth saving from drowning!)

Here are some simple rules:
   (1) Ask the person if you can do a quick survey "no strings attached." Let them know that you're not selling anything or recruiting for anything.
   (2) Tell them it will take less than 2 minutes.
   (3) Ask the questions and don't react to the answers unless there is an obvious need.
   (4) Write down their answers.
   (5) Thank them and let them go without preaching.
   (6) Pray silently for them. Be ready to pray audibly when it's appropriate.

Now that you understand it, you're probably willing to do it, especially if a friend does it with you. People who are outgoing and socially bold find it easier to get started. But if you're still scared to death, that's OK. There are other things you can do to touch people left of the cross.

3. Plan a Left-of-Cross Event.

These are a blast. They fall into three categories.

First, are **social** left-of-cross events. Twice a year, one of our church plants buys a block of tickets for the Seattle Mariners baseball game. They make this announcement on Sabbath: "A week from tomorrow, we're having a church social; we're all going to the baseball game. If you're willing to bring an unchurched friend, the church will pay for your ticket and theirs. How many of you would like to go and invite a friend?"

If you raise your hand, the church buys two tickets. If you bring your unchurched friend to the game, it costs you nothing. If you come alone or not at all, guess what? You just bought two tickets.

So while you're sitting at the game with your friend, what are you doing? Sure, you're cheering for the home team and hoping they make the playoffs this year. But what else are you doing? You're mingling. You're building a friendship with someone who needs Jesus, and praying that they will move one notch to the right. Eventually, you want them to find salvation. Can attending a baseball game be evangelism?

One Sabbath afternoon I was visiting in the home of a pastor. My cell phone rang. It was a church planter from Minnesota. "Hey, Ron! The first unchurched family just came to our party. I'm so excited, I had to slip outside and tell someone!"

"Cool, man! I'm delighted. Way to go!" I wished I was there to see it for myself.

Here's the background. Steven was planting a church that was a few months old. In spite of his nagging, the members would not invite their friends to the worship experience. When he asked them why, they hemmed & hawed, but finally admitted that they just weren't accustomed to inviting people to church. "Will you invite them to a party?" Steven asked. They all agreed, so Steven planned a party with a purpose.

Five minutes after the first call, my cell phone rang again. "The second unchurched family just came to our party. You should see how excited the people are who invited them!"

"Awesome! I'm proud of you."

Five minutes later, Steven called again. In fact, he was so pumped up that he called four times that afternoon to give me a progress report on their party. What did they do? Devoured food, of course. But after the meal, their music team played three songs to demonstrate what the music was like at church each Sabbath, their puppeteers did a short program for the kids, and they called it a night. Several unchurched people ended up attending church on a regular basis. Can a party qualify as evangelism?

When Matthew came to Jesus, he wanted to introduce his friends to Jesus. He wasn't very sure of himself and was afraid they would ask questions he couldn't answer, so he planned a party with a purpose and invited Jesus to come.[65] It worked.

One of our church plants holds Matthew parties with a different label. They call them "IP Parties." Here's the background. They moved into town to begin a "cold start" church (a church plant with no Adventist core group). Since there were no members, they had to start with non-members. Time after time they invited people to their home for a meal—neighbors, someone they met in the elevator, even strangers on the sidewalk. "Thanks, but I don't really know you" was a frustratingly typical response.

So they printed up some cards and headed out. "Hi, my name's Karen and I wonder if you'd like to come to an IP party!"

The person was surprised, but intrigued and curious. "Who are you and what, for heaven's sake, is an IP party?"

"We live over on 2nd Street and an IP party is an Interesting People party. We've had several of these. We meet the coolest people, and you look interesting—we'd love it if you could come to our next one!" Karen handed them an invitation card that says, "Interesting People Party. It's like meeting with friends you haven't met yet." On the card is the date, time and place.

It works. Many people who wouldn't be caught dead in a stranger's house somehow feel safe and welcome at an IP party. It's just a gimmick, but it offers a chance to get behind their defenses and build a friendship.

I asked the pastor if I was interesting enough to attend one of the parties. Forty-five minutes before the party started, what do you suppose we were doing? We were on our knees praying earnestly that God would bring the right people. That we could say the right things and avoid saying the wrong things. That the Holy Spirit would move everyone who came one notch closer to the cross. And what happened to us that night? We moved one notch to the right as well as God used us to bless someone else.

Second, are **Seasonal** left-of-cross events. Evangelistic churches take advantage of the times when people are most likely to visit a church—Easter and Christmas.

One of our church plants planned an "Easter Dessert Buffet." It was fabulous. The flickering light from a hundred candles illuminated a huge cross carved out of ice. Surrounding the cross was a display of desserts that would've made Martha

Stewart salivate. Floating lakes of carbonated punch, smoking with islands of dry ice, stood like guards over the cheesecake and the sorbet. Linen cloths smothered every table.

Two hundred people came to enjoy the evening, over half of whom were guests. When everyone had eaten, the music team led some worship songs. The pastor explained the death and resurrection of Jesus and shared his journey of coming to faith in Christ. He concluded with an appeal to follow Jesus as Savior. Can a dessert buffet be evangelism?

Third, are **spiritual** left-of-cross events. These are events that are overtly spiritual, but their intent is to connect with people and move them closer to the cross. Those who attend may eventually make a decision for baptism and church membership, but the purpose of this event is more limited.

One of our planters prepared a 7-night series and called it "Ancient Future." They advertised by distributing flyers and through personal invitation. Over a hundred people showed up and enjoyed creative topics like "Is That Your Final Answer?" and "Survivor—Would You Be Voted Off the Island?"

Three times a year, another church conducts a three- or four-night series called "Search Week." The topics are spiritual and tackle topics relevant to the unchurched in their community.

4. Experience the Fun of Servant Evangelism.
Servant evangelism is so fun it ought to be illegal. By definition, servant evangelism is doing organized acts of kindness with no strings attached to show God's love in a practical way. Here are a few examples.

Host a free car wash and don't accept donations. Everyone whose car is washed receives a card that says, "Yes, it really is free! It's a simple way of saying that God loves you, no strings attached." On the back side of the card is the church contact information.

Stake out a laundromat and wait for a young mother to struggle in with her mountain of laundry. Ask her, "Which machine would you like to use today? We're feeding the machines to show God's love." Plop in the quarters, and give her the contact card.

One of our Hispanic churches takes cold drinks to field workers on a hot day. When the weather is cold, they serve hot chocolate.

Nine Volt Evangelism

I was visiting a church plant in Oregon. "You've got to meet Dennis," the pastor insisted. "Make sure you talk with him after church."

"I was home watching football on Saturday afternoon," Dennis began. His face lit up like the birthday boy in a Norman Rockwell painting. "Someone knocked at my door. When I opened it, there stood a kid who handed me a 9 volt battery and a card. I wondered who on earth would try to sell batteries door to door, but he said 'It's free. We want to make sure your family is safe. Please check your smoke alarm,' and he vanished. Later that night, I called the number on the card and talked with the pastor. I invited him over, we started studies, and now I come here every week."

"So you came to church because of a battery?"

"Sure did," he said. "I had never heard of a church that gave things to people. I thought churches always wanted to get something out of me. When the pastor came over, I asked if I could visit his church. He told me I could come, but warned me that they meet at a different time than most churches. I didn't care. All I knew was here was a church that gives instead of trying to receive."

"Have you studied what Adventists believe?"

"I have now," Dennis announced. "The Sabbath is really cool. I never knew about that before, but now I'm getting ready to be baptized!" A few months later, Dennis was baptized.

Christmas Gift Evangelism

Several of our churches wrap gifts in the mall at Christmas time. You've seen different groups doing that and you know what they want – they always expect a donation. Not us. We who do servant evangelism have agreed not to accept donations under any conditions. Except one. If someone offers a million dollars or more, we'll accept it. Anything less than that, we won't take it. (Then again, anything in the 6-figure range would be tempting!)

A church plant in Wichita had arranged to wrap presents at their local mall. One gentleman laid his gift on the table and waited for it to be wrapped. When it was finished, he tried to pay for it.

"We're not accepting donations," the member said. "It's totally free."

The man insisted on paying. "Nothing's free," he said.

"God's grace is free and we're doing this to show God's love. Thanks for offering, but we won't accept your money."

The man argued, refused to accept something for free, and actually became agitated. When he realized he'd never win this argument, he opened his wallet, slapped down four $20 bills and dashed out the door before anyone could catch him. He paid $80 to have his gift wrapped because he wouldn't accept grace.

Evangelism in a Bottle

"Pastor, I'm afraid to hand bottled water to a stranger. I'm too introverted. I don't think I can participate."

"How about this? Will you hold the sign?"

"Sure," she said. "I think I can handle that!"

A church plant in Olympia, Washington was distributing cold water in the park on a hot, summer day. Shy Sarah held up a sign that said, "Free Drinks. No Donations Accepted." All around her, the members were giving away the bottles with the contact card attached. Behind her, a young man took a bottle. "Why are you doing this?" he asked the Adventist.

"To show God's love," the member smiled.

"Nobody ever loved me," the kid's eyes dropped and focused on nothing.

"God loves you." They sat on the grass and a gospel presentation followed. Sarah was holding the sign with tears running down her face as she listened to a young man give his heart to Jesus Christ. She was too shy to give out the water, but she was an evangelist in her own way.

Remember when Jesus says, "If you give a cup of cold water in my name, it's like giving it to me?"[66] Do you know what the Greek for cold water is in that passage? *Dietus Cokus.* Not really. But there is really nothing more exciting than getting together with a bunch of friends and serving your community through servant evangelism.[67]

Everyone can be an evangelist. A child washing headlights at a car wash is. The interior designer who decorates for "Search Week" is. The baseball fan who brings his buddy to the game is. As is the person who shares a Bible study. And, of course, the reaping specialist who preaches the truths of God's Word is an evangelist as well.

Here's my advice: Broaden your definition of evangelism. Evangelism can be and should be a perpetual lifestyle of imitating Jesus, which means spending Sabbath morning right of the cross, then praying and playing and working the rest of the week left of the cross with the intention of nudging someone closer to Christ and their eventual salvation.

As an individual Christian, do what Jesus did and hang out with people who need God's love. Corporately, plan a menu of church-initiated events designed to connect with people left of the cross and move them one notch to the right.

Every church stops growing when the price gets too high. Could this be part of your price?

And all the people said...

---

36   Matthew 9:36.

37   Acts 17:5a; The Message.

38   Acts 17:11, KJV.

39   Acts 17:22, The Message.

40   Ellen White, *Acts of the Apostles*, p. 241.

41   The Voice of the Martyrs website is www.persecution.com.

42   *Jesus Freaks*, Albury Publishing, p. 316.

43   From a private e-mail.

44   We see pockets of Berea in Athens, mainly immigrants—Hispanics in America, Islanders in England—but the majority population in First World countries do not readily respond to the gospel.

45   Paraphrase of Mark 6:11.

46   See Ellen White, *Testimonies*, Vol. 9, p. 189 and I Corinthians 9:19-23.

47   A new twist on evangelism in North America is to do the same thing as before but with a lay person reading a script and using prepared DVD graphics.

48   Extrapolated from research conducted by Donnelly Marketing Group. Reported in *Marketing for Congregations*, p. 190-195.

49   Adapted from the Engle Scale.

50   Barna Research Group reports that fewer than 3 out of 10 Americans even believe that there is such a thing as absolute truth.

51   John 14:12.

52   1 Corinthians 3:6.

53   John 4:34-35.

54   John 4:37-38.

55 *Review & Herald*, August 22, 1899.

56 David Newman, former editor of *Ministry* magazine, told me that his mother joined the Adventist church after an 18 month series of meetings.

57 Conversation with his daughter, Kathy Smith.

58 Thanks to Scott Cassell.

59 Authored by Rebecca Pippert.

60 Luke 19:10.

61 Robert Lewis, *The Church of Irresistible Influence*, p. 28.

62 See 2 Corinthians 5:18-20.

63 Mark 2:17.

64 Read also Ellen White, *The Desire of Ages*, p. 152 where she urges us to mingle with people on their turf.

65 See Luke 5:27-32.

66 Matthew 10:42.

67 For an exciting explanation of Servant Evangelism, read *Conspiracy of Kindness* and *101 Ways to Reach Your Community*, both by Steve Sjogren. Also, check out www.servantevangelism.com.

HABIT 5

THE WORSHIP
EXPERIENCE

W orship is the 'thank you' that refuses to be silenced.

—Max Lucado

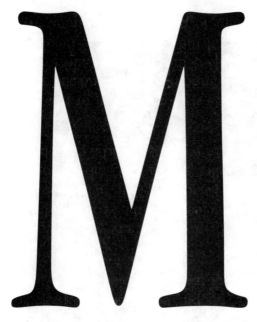

Most worship services begin at 11 o'clock sharp and end at 12 o'clock dull.

The boy was bored to tears. The church service seemed as if it would never end. His eyes were wandering around the room and settled on something he had never noticed before. He nudged his mother, pointed to the wall, and whispered, "Mommy, what's that?"

"It's a plaque," she whispered back.

"What's a plaque?"

"It's a list of everyone who died in the service."

The little guy was horrified. His face was frozen in stone. "Mommy, was that the early service or the late service?"

The worship experience is all too often a reason why churches stop growing. The pastor can organize plenty of ministry teams, the facility can be attractive and have plenty of space for expansion, relationships can be healthy, and the church members can all be evangelists, but if the worship is dead, the church will not reach the lost.

Adventists almost never invite their friends to church. For two reasons. First, they don't have any. They have non-Adventist acquaintances, but very few friends. Second, they're not sure if it's safe. If your Sabbath worship is to contribute to the growth of your church, three things must be true.

First, **believers can't wait to attend**. When they jump out of bed on Sabbath morning, they are eager to go to church. They know that they will enjoy what happens there, they will be challenged in their walk with Christ, and they will leave with their hearts filled with love for God.

All evangelistically effective churches have excellent worship. Members in those churches often use words like "Energy", "Relevance", and "Joy" to describe what happens. Ask yourself this question: *Why would I invite someone to something that I don't enjoy myself? If my kids consider it boring, if I consider it boring, why would I want to persecute someone else by bringing them here?*

Let's say your family is going camping next weekend. If the worship is consistently superb, someone in your family is going to say, "Hey, why don't we leave for the campground directly from church so we don't have to miss worship?" When people feel that way about your Sabbath worship, you're on the right track.

Second, **the members are proud to bring their friends**. Five times in 1 Corinthians 14, Paul speaks about unbelievers in the service. "But if an unbeliever comes in, he is convinced and, falling down on his face, he will worship God and report that God is truly among you."[68] It should be normal to see non-Adventist guests in every Sabbath worship event. Scripture teaches that we ought to plan the service with a deliberate sensitivity to those who are far left of the cross on the evangelism scale.

In the gospel of Matthew, Jesus says, "When anyone hears the word of the kingdom, and *does not understand it,* then the wicked one comes and snatches away what was sown in his heart."[69] Whose responsibility is it to make sure a person understands? It's ours. If we don't present the truths of the Bible so that the unbeliever understands, the wicked one will snatch away what was sown in his or her heart. And then someone will wrongly label them as uninterested or unspiritual.

Think of it like this: When we humans had a terrible problem of rebellion and alienation from God, He chose to see that as His problem rather than ours. Too often today, when some people find Christianity confusing or even offensive, the church responds by saying, "That's their problem. We are telling the truth. Too bad they're not interested in it."

I'm in good company (God's) when I disagree with that sentiment. We dare not see it as their problem; it is *our* problem. We are never free to change the content of the gospel, but in order to faithfully carry out the Gospel Commission, we have to knock ourselves out to make the good news as comprehensible as possible, just as Jesus did with His parables.

"If you have a light," Jesus asks, "why would you hide it under a tub so no one can see it?"[70] He answers His own question by presenting the most profound truths in simple, understandable ways. The very folks who wouldn't walk down the street to hear the Pharisees or the Sadducees were mesmerized by Jesus' teachings and they exclaimed, "Never a man spoke like this man!"[71]

When Adventists have friends who don't know Jesus, when they can't wait to attend church themselves on Sabbath, and they know that what happens in worship is planned with a deliberate sensitivity to unbelievers, they *will* invite their friends to church. The worship experience then becomes a powerful means of helping the lost take their next step toward the cross.

Third, **whoever attends is eager to return**. Your church's very best interest is a second-time guest. It's one thing to get someone through the door once; it's another to get them back. How do you do that?

Create an Experience

Notice that I call this habit "The Worship Experience." Not the worship service, but the worship experience. We live in an experience economy. A generation ago, Americans tried to keep up with the Joneses. We no longer have that quest because, with few exceptions, everyone already has everything. Instead, people today are in hot pursuit of the latest, greatest experience.

The Birthday Cake

When I was a boy, my mother had her hands full. She had eight children and was a full-time school teacher. Yet every year when my birthday rolled around, she took the time to go to the store and buy flour, cocoa, shortening, sugar and whatever else she needed to make a birthday cake—by hand, from scratch. She did the same for all my brothers and sisters. The ingredients cost 10-20 cents.

Fast forward to the '80s. When a child had a birthday, what did Mom do? She bought a cake mix from the grocery story with a Duncan-Hines or Betty Crocker label. She poured the mix in a bowl, stirred in some milk, cracked an egg or two, and popped it in the oven. It was faster and produced the same results as a hand-made cake. The mix cost a dollar or two, but the basic ingredients were still 10-20 cents.

Now accelerate to the '90s. What did a parent do when a kid's birthday arrived? She certainly didn't bake a cake from scratch; she didn't even snatch a cake mix off the shelf. That would take too long; she was just too busy for that. Instead, she ordered a cake from Safeway or Kroger—already made, custom decorated, and ready to eat. Without blinking at the cost, she paid ten or twenty dollars, but the basic ingredients were still 10-20 cents.

When a child has a birthday today, what happens? Mom and Dad take Junior to Chuck E. Cheese's with a dozen friends. They pig out on fries, ice cream and cake surrounded by decorations, entertainment and noise. The extravaganza costs one or two hundred dollars, but the basic ingredients of the cake still cost 10-20 cents.

What's happened? We live in an experience economy. Whether child or adult, we refuse to live in the past. Especially on the weekends, we invest our time and energy in experiences.

REI

Take a visit to REI, one of America's largest outdoor outfitters. Their flagship store is in Seattle, Washington. Enter the building and you've walked smack dab into the middle of an outdoor experience. Strap on some climbing gear and see if you have what it takes to achieve the pinnacle of the 65 foot, indoor climbing wall. Straddle a mountain bike and test the seat and the shocks on their bike track. Pick up an interpretive pamphlet to help kids learn which of those tracks on the floor came from a bear, a mountain lion, or a raccoon. In the Denver store, you can hang out in the cold room to find out if that jacket or sleeping bag has enough insulation to keep you warm. There's even a "demo dock" so you can plop your dream kayak in the water before taking it home. REI sells experiences.

The Mall of America

Perhaps America's greatest icon of the experience economy is the Mall of America in Bloomington, Minnesota. Seven Yankee stadiums would fit inside the 4.2 million square foot behemoth. Only 90,000 people live in Bloomington itself, yet more people visit the mall each year—43 million—than visit the Grand Canyon, Graceland, and Disney World combined.

Imagine 520 stores, more than 50 restaurants, and the Camp Snoopy amusement park with 30 rides. Add several nightclubs, the Lego Imagination center for children, a neon blue-hued bowling alley, a NASCAR motor speedway, and a 1.2 million gallon aquarium containing 65 sharks and 3,000 other creatures. Take a breath and try to picture a bank, a Northwest Airlines travel center, the nation's only full service Post Office in a mall, a dental clinic, medical clinic and the Sage Clinic which screens uninsured and underinsured women for breast and cervical cancer.

If you want to get married, you came to the right place. You can join the nearly 4,000 other couples who have tied the knot in the Chapel of Love. And you don't have to run all over town to get ready; you can rent tuxedos, buy wedding cake, bridesmaid dresses and photographic service all in the mall. And why not celebrate your reception in one of the restaurants?

Locals joke that you can buy apple pie, attend a wedding, and have a vasectomy while your kids ride the Ripsaw roller coaster and your wife studies accounting at National American University. And if Lego World didn't tire them out, your kids may persuade you to visit the world's largest turtle collection —right in the mall.

Someone estimated that it would take you 3-4 days just to visit all of the stores and attractions. Yet amazingly, developers plan to double the mall to over 10 million square feet. Virtually no one goes to the Mall of America to buy things; they go for the experience. Then they buy things to commemorate what they've experienced. People in First World countries expect an experience.

The Dinosaur Museum

Pretend you own a museum. Your marquee exhibit is a skeleton of a Tyrannosaurus Rex from Minsk, Russia. It was discovered under 2,000 feet of molten rock and meticulously excavated and reconstructed by paleontologists. The cost of bringing this rare and fabulous specimen to your museum was enormous.

You have it on display in a towering, 120 foot-high Plexiglas case that keeps the temperature and humidity just right. Next to the rail that prevents people from getting too close is an interpretive sign explaining that the old creature roamed the earth during the Mesozoic Era. Curious visitors pause for a moment before the gigantic frame, mutter their comparisons with the creatures from the movie *Jurassic Park*, and move right along, unaffected by the incredible archeological wonder of faceless jaws hovering a dozen stories above.

Across the street is the "Dinosaur Experience." In the lobby is a T-Rex made out of plastic for several thousand dollars. Its jaws are the size of six children's heads. Instead of a rail and a security guard, a museum photographer records your child's face as she pokes her head inside the sound-enhanced, gnashing jaws, imagining what it would be like if, instead of coming here for lunch, she came here as dinner.

Which museum will prove to be the most successful? It's no contest. Why? Because people demand an experience. Most secular organizations have figured this out while the church often lags behind. "The children of the world," Jesus lamented, "are wiser than the children of the light."

Worship Worth Celebrating

Churches can no longer do worship according to the 1952 radio model and expect to grow.[72] Doing church with a passive and silent audience appeals to the older generation but fails to reach those raised in the TV and Internet era. There are a myriad of appropriate ways to create a Sabbath morning experience that (a) immerse people in God's Word, (b) connect them with God and with one another, and (c) encourage participation.

"But wait just a minute!" I can hear someone exclaim. "It sounds to me like you're promoting celebration worship."

I was pastoring a church in Wisconsin and was attending the summer camp meeting. An elder from one of the churches cornered me and spit out a question. The hostile expression on his face would've scared a freight train off the tracks. "I've heard that you are a celebration pastor and that your church is a celebration church. Is that true?" He was apparently referring to the five or six worship songs before the message each Sabbath and the occasional parable-in-action.

His definition and mine of "celebration" were no doubt different, but I decided this was a chance for some fun and some teaching.

"You've heard correctly," I smiled. "We are a celebration church. But here's a question for you: Isn't your church a celebration church?"

"Absolutely not!" He was as testy as a coiled serpent.

"It's not?" I aggravated him to make a point. "Maybe I should have a talk with your pastor. You see, the Bible says that all of our churches should be celebration churches."

"There's no such text." The forceful sweep of his arm could have felled a tree.

"Leviticus 23:32. 'From evening until evening shall you celebrate the Sabbath.'" The text rolled off my tongue as if I had rehearsed it. "The entire Sabbath should be celebration, but especially the worship experience."

It struck him funny. His grin temporarily erased the crease from his forehead. We shook hands and agreed to continue the conversation later. Ellen White's comment could have helped him: "The scenes of Calvary call for the deepest emotion. Upon this subject you will be excusable if you manifest enthusiasm."[73]

Worship as Entertainment

Obviously, anything can go too far, even something good. So how do you find the balance? When does worship deteriorate into commotion that doesn't feed the soul and fails to honor God?

Consider three words. First, *amusement.* Is amusement acceptable in worship? Cut the word apart. The core of the word is "muse" which means "to ponder" or "to think." The letter "a" at the first of the word means "not to." (For example, "amoral" means "not moral.") The word amusement literally means "not to think" or "not to ponder." With that understanding, I would argue that amusement may be OK in other contexts, but is not acceptable in worship.

The second word is *entertainment.* What does the word mean? The dictionary says, in part:
(a) Hospitality; hospitable provision for the wants of a guest
(b) That which engages the attention agreeably.[74]

If our family entertains yours as guests, we do everything possible to be hospitable and to engage your attention. Our house may be cluttered during the week, but before you arrive, we'll take out the trash and vacuum the floors. We'll find out what you like to eat. Is there anything you don't eat? What time is best for you to eat? And when the meal is over, you can count on me to ask if you'd like to watch my slides. If you would, I'll be glad to plug in the old projector and dim the lights. If you prefer not to, we'll do something else because we take entertainment seriously.

Entertainment means "to hold a person's attention." Certainly we should hold people's attention in worship. Entertainment in worship, then, is acceptable.

But I think there's an even better word: *Edu-tainment*,[75] where we connect the worshipper with God in an atmosphere that teaches them eternal truths while holding their attention.

Ellen White experienced what most traveling preachers endure: way too many boring Sabbaths. "Our services should be intensely interesting,"[76] she insists. *Intensely interesting.*

Give yourself a test. Cross-examine yourself in regard to last Sabbath's worship. On a scale of one to ten, how interesting was it? One means boring and dry. Ten means, well, *intensely* interesting. How did you do?

Now do it again, this time looking through the eyes of a first-time guest to an Adventist church. How intensely would last Sabbath's service engage his or her attention? If you're not sure, find a first-time guest and ask him or her.

Who Fits in Your Worship?

If your church creates an awe-inspiring worship experience Sabbath after Sabbath, things will begin to change in some positive ways. You'll tend to attract the younger generation. Creative people will come out of the woodwork to offer their ideas and their help. And most everyone will look forward to Sabbath.

But there's not just one way to do worship. No book or committee can prescribe an order of service or style of music that meets everyone's needs. So how should you plan? If you want to move believers closer to God while being sensitive to unbelieving guests, what rules should guide the worship planning team?

Let's start with this: Some people will attend your church every time the doors are open. No matter what you do, you can count them as present before they even arrive. They may not always *like* what you do, but they will fill a seat every single week.

Everyone else, especially younger believers and pre-Christian guests, will analyze what you do in an effort to decide whether or not they fit in your worship experience. Assuming they've decided to check it out, here are six things that will bring them back or keep them away.

Music

To discuss church music is to pick a fight, but since God invented music, and music is crucial to worship and to reaching lost people, let's try to discuss it and see if we remain friends.

Suppose you've been invited to lead music at a nursing home on Sabbath afternoon. What kind of music will you do? Old hymns, sung slowly. Between songs there'll be a break so you can assist the residents in finding the next hymn. At least that's what I would do.

The next Sabbath, you're asked to lead music at your conference youth camp for the young people. Will the music there differ from the music at the old folks' home? I hope so. If it doesn't, what will happen? The teenagers will vote with their feet and disappear while someone laments that "today's young people just don't care about God." Is that true? Not at all. You were insensitive to their needs. You drove them away.

Now let's flip over the coin. You lead music for the young people first, then the next week you do, at the nursing home, what you did at the youth camp. (*I like bananas, I think that mangos are sweet, I like papayas, but nothing can beat, the sweet love of God!*) What will happen? The old people who are able, will shuffle away with their walkers or ride down the hall in their wheelchairs while someone laments that "today's older people just don't care about God." That isn't true. You were insensitive. You drove them away.

Here's the deal. If you can't do music on Sabbath afternoon to meet the needs of all groups of people, what makes you think you can on Sabbath morning? You really can't, but you do have these options: (a) Try to find a happy middle ground by blending the old with the new, (b) Offer two Sabbath worship experiences, each with a different music style. But whatever you do, remember that everything you do must be relevant and understandable to a first-time guest.

In her book *Evangelism*, Ellen White says, "Do not sing funeral hymns."[77] If you ignore her advice—as all-too-many churches do—you'll appeal to those who expect to be embalmed in the near future. If you sing older hymns, you will attract those who were raised with a strong Christian heritage. If your music is contemporary, you will reach younger people who are searching, but who may or may not understand or relate to Christian lingo. Remember that all music was contemporary when it was written.

I was bored one day and decided to research our hymn book. Here's what I discovered. Fourteen percent of the songs in the

Adventist hymnal use language like we speak today. Forty-two percent use language with Christian symbolism, but even without a Christian background, you can figure out the meaning. But 44 percent of the songs in our hymnal use language so heavy with Christian symbolism that a non-Christian wouldn't even know the meaning of the words. The apostle Paul would counsel us today, "If you're going to sing in tongues, by all means, have an interpreter."[78]

Your style of music will define who attends your church. In established churches, the natural tendency is to do music to please the older generation. Which likely explains two things. First, why unchurched guests are rare in Adventist churches. Second, why the average age in the United States is 35 while the average Adventist is 53. We have kept our hymnals but lost our children.

Drama and the Arts
Michelangelo did not use a paint-by-numbers kit from *Toys R Us* to paint the Sistine Chapel. God wired him up with a brain that could transfer the astonishing beauty he saw in his mind to the canvas or the plaster. For some reason that's beyond me, God has endowed certain people with a liberal dose of creativity. Does your church value their gifts? Are artistic people urged to honor God and build up the church by serving according to their giftedness?

Creativity is the 5th word in the Bible, yet whenever we address this topic, we plunge head first into controversy. Some people believe that any type of creative expression in the worship service is a sin, while others find that it enhances their worship and prepares their heart for the message. Ellen White's view was that drama itself is neutral. Like music, the sermon, or any other element of worship, it can be used either for good or for bad.[79]

Some churches use video clips to illustrate Bible truths. Others perform a song while someone signs with their hands. One church places several flip charts on the platform and asks the youth to draw what they are hearing as the pastor presents the message.

If you choose to use drama and the arts in worship, you will attract creative people who don't attend church because they've been told that their gifts are inappropriate in church. Those who have strong feelings against the use of the arts may stay away because their view of church is more traditional. The choice you make will determine which group fits in your church. And when creative people enjoy church, they are likely to influence their circle of friends to join them.

Technology

Most churches are far behind the rest of society when it comes to technology; if the organ uses electricity, they consider themselves on the cutting edge. Secular people who surf the Internet, store data in a palm pilot, watch DVD movies, or tinker with the latest digital camera will not attend a church that lives in the past.

In virtually every church, there's a young person or two who would be delighted to put the announcements and the songs on PowerPoint. If someone asked them, they would love to illustrate the pastor's message. If the people in the neighborhoods you hope to reach are technologically literate, your church must be as well.

Excellence

As a pastor, I have conducted dozens of weddings and learned that rehearsals are serious business. It's supremely important that everything happens just right. The coordinator sticks tape on the floor so the attendants stand in a perfect "V". The music changes when the mother stands, or was it the mother stands when the music changes? The bride hands her flowers to the

Maid of Honor at precisely the right moment. And on and on it goes for sometimes two hours or more, because it's a wedding and it's important that everyone does everything just right.

But when it comes to church, we seldom worry too much about it because—hey!—it's just God. So the sound system squeals. The pianist plays with mittens on. *The Mission Spotlight* slides are all in backwards. The soloist apologizes because he didn't have time to practice or his throat is sore. And people who visit are distracted and confused as to why the worship of God is taken so lightly.

Professional people attend seminars at work where the room is attractive and clean, the receptionists are pleasant and efficient, the sound system is adjusted ahead of time, and the presentation is well-prepared and illustrated. Especially if you expect to reach middle and upper-middle class people, every part of your worship service must be presented with excellence. God instructed the Israelites long ago, "Don't bring a blemished lamb. When you come to worship God, bring Him your best."[80] He would say the same today.

Dress

You only have to travel overseas a few times to realize that dress standards are largely cultural. I worshiped in one country where the men wore "dresses" and the ladies wore slacks to church. In other countries, a man is required to wear a necktie if he calls for or collects the offering.

Once we understand that dress is cultural, we live by two principles for Sabbath dress. The first is modesty. The second is to wear clothes that are attractive, clean, and culturally appropriate.

What about neckties? Is God offended when a man shows up to church without wearing one? No. Neckties are not mandated in the Bible. (What color necktie did Jesus wear?) They are clearly cultural in some settings while in others, a man would stick out like a sore thumb if he wore one. Have you read the text that tells pastors not to wear a necktie in hot weather? "Moses commanded the people saying, 'The priest shall not wear anything that causes sweat.'"[81]

My dad used to wear a tie to the grocery store, on vacation, and at the Saturday night social. So did most other men in his era. Today, it is possible to dress appropriately with or without one. Since it's not a matter of salvation, it becomes an issue of preference. More important, of course, is to make sure that unbelievers don't feel awkward because they don't fit our dress code. We have to make them feel welcome without compromising Biblical principle.

I conducted a reaping series in a small Missouri town. When I covered the Sabbath truth, I invited the guests to church. "Oh, I can't come," one of the ladies told me. "My husband and I are farmers and I don't even own a nice dress. I'm sure the other ladies will wear their Sunday best and I'll feel out-of-place."

"No problem," I told her. "Just wear slacks. There will be ladies at church who are not wearing dresses." She was skeptical at first, but she agreed to attend.

I went home and told my wife, "I want you to go to church this Sabbath in slacks instead of a dress." When I explained the reason, she grinned, grabbed the phone and called the head elders' wife. "Hey Susan," she said, "You're not allowed to wear a dress to church this Sabbath. Here's why..." They both laughed and showed up at church in attractive slacks.

When the lady visited church that week, she was delighted. "You were right," she told me, surprised that I had told her the truth. "I'm not the only female without a dress!" A few weeks later, I baptized both her and her husband.

Someone always asks, "Doesn't Ellen White tell us to wear our best to church?" Yes. But let's consider the context of her counsel. She was speaking to farmers who rose early, milked their cows, then showed up in church smelling like the barn. "Honor God," she pleads. "Have mercy on the saints. Wear your best to church." If I wore my best clothes to church today, I would not wear a suit and tie. The best I have is my $350 North Face mountain climbing jacket.

The way your leaders dress on Sabbath will determine who feels comfortable in your church. Churches where everyone wears formal clothes feel exclusionary to a secular person, especially if they are young. Never compromise principle, but do everything you can to make the unbeliever feel welcome in your church.

The Sermon

A group of young people were planting a church and asked me to consult with them. They were still in the process of developing their business plan and they wanted me to help them tweak their vision. Listen from the sidelines to part of the conversation.

Joan: "One thing I feel strongly about is that we shouldn't preach the prophecies in our new church. We're targeting unchurched people, and those beasts and all that stuff are scary. So let's agree not to preach any of the prophecies."

Jim: "I'm totally with you. In fact, I don't think we should preach any doctrines at all. We can teach those somewhere else, but the kind of people we're going to reach don't really need the doctrines, they need Jesus."

John: "Sounds good to me. But I'll take it one step further. I don't think we should have any sermons at all in our new church. Post-modern Americans don't like to listen to a talking head. They like to hang out and make friends. Let's agree that we're not going to have sermons in the church."

"Well, what on earth will we do?" Someone's outburst saved me from asking.

John again: "Let's do hot music, cool drama, serve drinks, and sit around tables discussing issues. I'm sure people will come to that."

I was praying. What on earth was I going to say to this well-meaning gang of young people to get them back on track? An illustration came to mind I had never thought of before.

"How many of you have heard of Jerry Garcia?" I knew he was from my generation, but I hoped they could relate.

"He was the lead singer with the Grateful Dead." Someone closer to my age remembered. "He's dead now, himself, but everyone knows Jerry."

"You got it," I was off to a good start. "I want you to think about something. Let's pretend Jerry is still around. He and his band show up in your town next weekend. What will happen?"

"Thousands of people will come to the concert." I thought I heard someone say *Duh!*

"Right on," I acknowledged. "But let's say Jerry and band do a concert in the same place in your town ten weeks in a row. What would happen?"

"The crowd would start to dwindle, I suppose." Only one of them spoke, but they were all with me.

"What if Jerry Garcia and the Grateful Dead came to this town and did their thing 52 weeks in a row. What would happen?" I had them and they knew it.

"They wouldn't have much of a crowd. They'd have a handful of 'Dead Heads' and that's about it."

I pounced on the moral like a rat on a Cheeto. "There is no entertainer anywhere who can hold a crowd week after week after week. That's why they come into town for a few days, then blast on to the next city. I don't care if it's Madonna, Michael Jackson or the Heralds, no musician or band will bring back a crowd indefinitely.

"If you expect people to come to church just to hear your music," I continued, "you'll be disappointed. If they want to hear music, they'll pop in a CD. It's better quality than what you can do. The unchurched will not crawl out of bed on Sabbath morning to watch your drama. They can get a lot better drama on television by watching a re-run of *Seinfeld* or *Friends* or whatever show is hot today. If they want to sit around tables and talk, they'll go to Starbucks.

"Your music is important; do the best you can. If you use drama, do it well. Create every opportunity you can to connect people with one another. But there is one primary thing that will bring the people back week after week and it's found in 1 Corinthians 1:21. It's called the foolishness of preaching." Thankfully, they were listening. "Present God's word in a clear, compelling way with a deliberate sensitivity to those you're trying to reach, because the Word of God alone has the power to bring people to Christ and to keep them there."

Five-minute Preaching Class

In the first chapter, I asserted that growing churches always have excellent preaching. And I promised to tell you how virtually anyone can become an excellent preacher. Here's my five-minute preaching class. It consists of two rules.

Rule #1: Preach with internal passion

Let me contrast two well-known Adventist preachers. The first is Ron Halvorson. Ron is one of the most energetic preachers I have heard. He epitomizes what I call "aerobic preaching." He paces from one side of the stage to the other. He sweats like marathon runner and mops up the sweat with a folded hankie. I've seen him rip off his tie, toss his jacket over the pew and preach his heart out. And everyone is on the edge of his or her seat.

The other preacher is Morris Venden. Give him a pulpit and you know where he'll stand. He rests his hands in the same place the entire time. The extent of his movement is a subtle rocking from side to side. His voice is calm and his tone rarely changes. And everyone is on the edge of his or her seat.

What makes both men exceptional preachers? It's obviously not their style. It's what I call internal passion. I'll define it with this story.

Almost every Friday afternoon, my cell phone rings; I might be in an airport or riding in my car. No matter where I am, my friend, Dave, gives me a call. I always drop everything because his enthusiasm pumps me up.

"Hey, Ron! Do you have a minute? Let me tell you about my sermon tomorrow. I'm preaching on the 3rd commandment and I'm starting with this story!" Verbs and nouns flow out of his mouth like a tape player on fast forward. "Then I'm going to tell them…" (and he reels off the points in his sermon). "But wait 'til you hear my conclusion!" and he preaches the conclusion. In three or four minutes, I hear the highlights of a 40 minute message.

At first I thought it was weird. *Why is he preaching his sermon to me?* I wondered. Then I went to hear him preach.

When Dave stands up to preach, he *knows* that what he is about to say, God has told him to say. It's so important that he just can't wait until Sabbath morning to preach it to the saints —which is why he calls me on Friday afternoon. He has to share it with someone, and that someone is me. His members love his preaching because he speaks with internal passion.

What is internal passion? It's the rock-solid conviction that what you're about to say is absolutely vital for everyone to hear. You *know* God gave it to you and you can hardly wait to say it. Ron Halvorson has internal passion. Morris Venden has internal passion. Pastor Dave has internal passion.

How do you get it? You spend time on your knees. You prepare a simple, clear and compelling message. You speak from a heart that's in love with God and you know that God will use His word to save someone's soul.

Rule #2: Preach to Two People

Don't worry about anyone else in the audience. Preach to two people: Someone who is hearing the gospel for the very first time, and someone who is hearing the gospel for the very last time.

Preach with internal passion and preach to two people, and you'll be an excellent preacher. People will be on the edge of their seats. When unbelievers worship with you, they'll get in the car after the service and say, "That was good. I learned something new about God today. Now I have hope. Now I know how to deal with mom's cancer or with that difficult person at work. I'll bet there's more where that came from. I'm coming back next week."

Combine it with the right music, integrate the arts, employ technology, do the best you can with what you have, and the foolishness of preaching will bring them back time after time after time.[82]

Here's the bottom line. Worship has everything to do with whether or not your church will reach the lost. What happens on Sabbath—your congregation's form of worship and style of music—will inevitably be linked to your mission. Ask yourself honestly, *What is our mission? Is it primarily to (a) serve current Adventist members and their children? Or (b) make the gospel attractive to those who will not go to heaven unless something changes between now and Jesus' coming?*

If your answer is (a), your worship can be nostalgic and exclusive. If your answer is (b), do whatever it takes to make your worship welcoming and inclusive for believer and unbeliever alike.

Every church stops growing when the price gets too high. Does your worship experience contribute to the growth of your church or is it a hindrance? If so, keep it up. If not, your price is clear.

---

11 Assumptions for Adventist Worship[83]

1) The goal of worship is to focus on the greatness of God rather than on ourselves or our needs.

2) The result of worship must be healing and power for living transformed lives. It must bring us into closer relationship with Jesus and with other worshipers, and then challenge us to purposeful service in the world.

3) Worship must clearly tell the story of Jesus Christ as our only hope and must show how His story can become ours.

4) Worship must examine and affirm what we as Seventh-day Adventists believe about God.

5) Because worship is an offering to God, it must be taken seriously and done with excellence.

6) Each worship experience must be carefully and purposefully planned.

> 7) Each element of worship is important and must contribute to the goal of that particular service.
>
> 8) The atmosphere of worship must include celebration, contemplation and commitment.
>
> 9) Worship must be participative for all present, not a performance for spectators.
>
> 10) Each worship experience must be intensely interesting and take advantage of the curious power of variety.
>
> 11) Each aspect of worship must be understandable and useful for the first-time guest.

68   1 Corinthians 14:24-25.

69   Matthew 13:19.

70   Paraphrase of Matthew 5:15.

71   John 7:46.

72   See Lyle Schaller, *What Have We Learned?*, p. 23.

73   Ellen White, *Testimonies*, Vol. 2, p. 213.

74   www.dictionary.com.

75   Leonard Sweet, *Soul Tsunami*, p. 213.

76   Ellen White, *Testimonies*, Vol. 9, p. 233.

77   Page 122.

78   Paraphrase of 1 Corinthians 14:5.

79   For a study on Ellen White and Drama, contact the EG White Estate at 301-680-6540.

80   Paraphrase of Leviticus 22:21 and Deuteronomy 15:21.

81   Ezekiel 44:18.

82   For some additional advice on preaching, read "The Ten Commandments of Communication" by Walt Kallestad in his book *Turn Your Church Inside Out*, p. 93-109.

83   The video series "Permission to Worship" is based on these 11 assumptions. Available from Advent*Source*.

HABIT 6

THE STRUCTURE

*B*rilliant ideas spill from thousands of pulpits
every Sunday, destined for a quick, premature
death. Why? Because only structure, well thought-
out structure, which effectively unleashes people
with purpose, can get results.

—Robert Lewis

The undisputed heavyweight of management theory is Peter Drucker. "The purpose of organization," he declares, "is to make weaknesses irrelevant."[84] A logical and efficient organizational structure is mandatory. When your church organizes properly, it minimizes its weaknesses while maximizing its strengths. The result is powerful.

Here's what you're after. You want a church where everyone gets loved, everyone gets to serve, and all that you do is focused on bringing as many as you can to the cross. Once you reach them, you journey together one notch at a time (picture the evangelism scale) with the goal of becoming definitely devoted disciples.

It's not OK when people are hurting and they can't find support. It's not OK when people want to serve and they don't know how. And it's not OK when year after year few, if any, find Christ through the ministry of the church. We learned earlier from Acts 6 that if you fail to organize properly, your effectiveness will grind to a halt.

God has graciously given every Christ-follower two things: (a) spiritual gifts; (b) an unquenchable passion to use those gifts to build the kingdom. Because of inadequate or even counterproductive structures, a lot of energy, time and talent is squandered in the church. People who would knock themselves out for the cause—with a smile on their face—try for a while, but often throw in the towel when they see that their efforts hardly matter. They would love to honor God by making a difference, but they feel frustrated, hindered, hamstrung.

As you've no doubt concluded by now, a church can actually do the other six habits quite well, yet not grow. Right here is the reason. They are structured for decline or, at best, numerical plateau.

The Importance of Design

You've decided to build a house. With a kaleidoscope of emotions, you take a drive to the lumberyard. "I'd like to order some lumber," you announce to the guy at the counter. A patch, embroidered on his shirt, says Bob.

"That's what we sell," he grins. "What's your project?"

"Oh, the wife and I decided to build a house." You stand tall, your back as straight as a tree.

"Great. Let's take a look at your plans." Bob sweeps aside his coffee cup, a scribble pad and a few stray pens.

"Oh, we don't really have any plans," you admit. "We decided to bypass the architect and the blueprints and all that stuff. Figured we'd save a few bucks. Just give us the average amount of wood. You know, for a medium-sized house. We need plywood, two-by-fours, and trusses. Then we'll need wiring, windows, and shingles."

"Just the average amount," Bob mutters. He's incredulous but tries hard to hide it. "Just a minute." He punches a button on his phone. "Hey boss, I have a situation here and I need your assistance."

Somehow you talk them into delivery. There it stands at the end of the cul-de-sac: an average amount of wood, metal, glass and vinyl, everything you need to build your house. And perched on top are rolls of insulation like sleeping bags at a slumber party.

Are you serious? What kind of house will you have?

It isn't a stretch to say that this is how many churches design their structure. Not the building, of course, but the internal structure of the church, the way things are organized. Being intentional about a blueprint doesn't even cross their minds. And the result is chaos. God brings together all the materials the church needs to accomplish His will in the community— the Bible calls that material "living stones"[85]—but the church is seldom organized to fit it all together.

If the church is to be evangelistically effective, the pastor must be an architect. The church leaders must work with the pastor to create a design that makes weaknesses irrelevant, maximizes strengths, and releases the gifts and passion of the members. And it must always be flexible enough to allow the church to grow to the next level.[86]

Ye Ole Computer

My wife and I were married a few years B.C. (Before Computers)—at least no one we knew had a computer in their home. Fran was a travel agent on commission with her own clientele of business travelers and semi-often vacationers. In order to find flight, hotel and car rental prices, she had to call a gazillion toll-free numbers, confirm the details with the customer, then write out the paper tickets by hand. Keeping track of her clients required a legal pad, some file folders and a stack of index cards.

It was a Sunday morning. Fran extracted the five-pound newspaper from its plastic bag and began to sort it into "must read" and "couldn't care less." Somehow her eye caught an ad for a personal computer; Radio Shack was selling something called a Tandy computer. "Look at this!" she exclaimed with all the enthusiasm of someone who had just discovered a way to save time, decrease effort and make more money.

"They're just a gimmick," I did my best to dissuade her. Unsolicited logic spilled out of me with amazing ease. "I can't imagine giving up a month's salary for a something that we would hardly ever use."

Her imagination was more robust; she *could* imagine such a scenario with no difficulty whatsoever. And it wasn't long until she prevailed.

The Tandy had no hard drive. The DOS operating system was on a floppy disk the size of a tea plate. Each program was on a separate floppy and storage was barely sufficient for saving a few word documents. It processed information at the speed of a receding glacier. Whether starting up or saving a file, it groaned pathetically like an old man begging for a few more breaths. But it wasn't long until everyone in our family—even me—realized that a computer was indispensable.

Today's computers are different. Compared to the old Tandy, my Dell has literally 10,000 times the memory and 500 times the speed. And it's small enough to tuck under my arm or slide in and out of my computer case when I undergo security screening at the airport.

A computer is comprised of four components. First is the hardware—the actual screen, keyboard and body of the computer itself. Second is the software which contains the programs you want to run. Then there's the power source which comes from either the wall outlet or the built-in battery. Last is something that is virtually invisible but utterly fundamental to a functioning computer: the operating system.

Pretend you have three computers in your house. One is the old Tandy which you no longer use and is destined for the Smithsonian museum. (Mine ended up in a Wisconsin landfill many years ago.) Another is an old desktop with Windows 95. The other is the latest, greatest and fastest laptop money can buy.

Now make believe that it's Christmas and your kids receive a really cool computer game. *Exceptional graphics!* the cover claims. *You'll think you're actually there!*

As soon as the last gift is unwrapped, they want to try it out. "Run it on the old Tandy," you tell them, a teasing smirk on your face. You know better and so do they. The Tandy only takes 5 1/4 inch floppy disks and the software is on a CD. Your laptop is off-limits to them except when they're supervised so they try it on the Windows 95. What happens? It either crashes or, at best, runs so slowly that it won't take long for the kids to get exasperated and demand access to your laptop. "OK, kids," you acquiesce. "You can use my laptop." Their new game operates perfectly.

These four components correspond to the components in a church. The hardware is the building, grounds and other physical assets of the church. The software is the programs your church offers such as worship, Sabbath School, small groups and Pathfinders. The power source is God. But invisible is the operating system, the manner in which the church is organized. The systems and structures that allow the programs to operate efficiently. If you don't update it from time to time, your programs will sputter or even crash, and the church begins its journey toward decline.[87]

Two Extremes

As with most anything, there are two extremes to church structure. At one end of the spectrum, the church structure is so rigid that passion is stifled. The church board becomes a bottleneck to anything that hints of progress. Even people who excel in the marketplace are not allowed to start a new ministry or improve an existing one until permission is granted. "We've never done it that way before" is the unvoted mantra of the church.

Rick Warren is clear: "Every church must eventually decide whether it is going to be structured for control or structured for growth."[88] And William McKnight, former CEO of 3M Corporation says, "If you put fences around people, you get sheep."

The other extreme—a weak or non-existent structure—has the same effect: creativity is neutralized and fervor burns low if it burns at all.

A pastor once told me, "We don't worry about being organized. We just tell everyone to go ahead and do whatever God has placed on their heart."

"How's it working?" I asked. I'm pragmatic. If it works, I'm for it.

His answer was instructive. "Well, good and bad. We have a lot of things starting up, but they don't seem to last too long. We don't worry about it, though, because it's not long 'til something new pops up somewhere."

"How's the growth in the church? Numerical growth and spiritual growth." I went for the bottom line.

"Not too good," he owned up. "But our leaders like it because it saves them time."

"How's that?" I wondered.

"We don't have any regular meetings. The only thing that happens at the same time around here is our worship service and rehearsal for worship." He was proud to defend his position.

"You don't have board meetings or leadership meetings on a regular basis?" I asked.

"No, no, no. If something comes up, we call a quick meeting after church or we set up a conference call on the phone."

Here's what I told him. "If you want to make sure that your church stays small, you're doing everything right. That's the way you run a family. And it works pretty well when there's only Dad, Mom and a couple of kids. But if you want your church to grow, you have to be organized accordingly.

"For example," I continued, "we don't have a budget committee for our family. We have a budget, but my wife and I sit down and hammer out a draft, get some feedback from the kids, then we're done. We don't have a transportation committee. When our kids were teenagers, we had three cars and often needed to go in four directions. We discussed it at supper and the next morning everyone knew what car would take them where. We decided on Saturday night where and when to go on our next vacation, not through a committee.

"But imagine if I had 200 kids. Now I could use a budget committee, a transportation committee, a vacation committee. The need to be organized is exponentially greater with a couple hundred kids.

"Now think about the church. What if 200 people attend but you want to reach more? The importance of designing a structure that actually facilitates that is crucial." I know his head was convinced; I wasn't sure about his heart.

Let's leave the pastor behind and move on. Suppose you're convinced that the larger and more effective you intend your church to be, the more important your structure. Now what? How do you design a church structure that assures that everyone gets loved, everyone gets to serve, and the church continues to reach the lost? It's really quite simple. Here is a three-level structure that would make Peter Drucker proud. It makes weaknesses irrelevant in a church of 20, a church of 2,000, and every size in between.

Three Levels of Structure

Leadership Team
The first level is simple. Many churches call this level the church board; I prefer to call it the leadership team. Why? Its purpose is to lead. Not primarily to keep the machinery running, but to proactively discover ways to lead the congregation to achieve its maximum redemptive potential.

Remember what I said earlier about the pastor as leader? He (or she) seeks God's vision for the church. He paints a picture of a desirable future, then inspires and organizes people to step into that picture. The leadership team is an extension of that. The members of the team come alongside the pastor and, through prayer, help to shape and clarify the vision. They partner with him to light a fire in the hearts of the members. And finally, they synergize their experience and their resources—they do whatever it takes—to shape the future of the church.

As mentioned above, all too many church boards function as a veto to anything new or different. Or they delay an innovative ministry with reels of red tape until the person with a passion gives up on the church and invests his or her time building a boat or volunteering at Habitat for Humanity. In many churches, so-called leaders grab onto power like a pit bull on a cat's tail. Their need for control is a dead giveaway that their heart is spiritually corrupt. Their sin is self-centeredness.

Philosophically then, the leadership team does everything it can to create a climate where the answer is *Yes.* When someone has an idea that is consistent with the vision of the church, the leadership team finds a way to support it.

As part of a project, I was assigned to study *Heartland Community Church,* a fast-growing church in the Midwest. Some friends and I attended the service on Sunday. The place was packed.

One of the announcements went like this: "As you came in this morning, you noticed the construction equipment in the parking lot. No, we're not having a sale. We're not auctioning off machines for farmers. Actually, we're going to expand! You can see that we're packed to the walls. When we started this church four years ago, we promised that we would never allow anything to get in the way of reaching more people for Christ. Either we're done growing, or we have to enlarge our facilities.

"So tomorrow morning, those machines are going to start scraping dirt, digging holes, and making a mess. When you come next weekend—in fact, for the next six months or so—our parking lot will be a lot smaller. If you're a regular attender here at Heartland, do us a favor. Please park across the road and walk over here so our guests can park up close to the church."

Tuesday morning, five of us Adventists met with the pastoral staff for three hours. As soon as I could, I asked the pastor,[89] "Hey Mark, you made the announcement on Sunday that you were going to expand the facility. How did this church make that decision? Did you have a congregational meeting where they voted that?"

Mark looked at me like I was from Mars. "No, our leadership team made that decision."

"In our churches," I explained, "we don't make any decision like that without what we call a business meeting."

"Why on earth would you do that?" he waited for a moment but I didn't answer.

"Let me explain something," he went on. "When you require approval for a decision from the whole congregation, you risk lowering the vision to the level of the person who has the least amount of faith. Many people who attend those meetings never pray. They aren't seeking God daily on their knees. They aren't spending time hanging out with lost people. They don't give a rip if their neighbors go to heaven or hell. Why would you let them influence the future of the church? When you open up the decision to the entire church, you allow people to make speeches and to vote who aren't even spiritual. You could never move forward boldly if you did that!"

John Maxwell explains it this way: "If you're following twelve cars up a curvy, two-lane, mountain road, how fast do you drive? As fast as the slowest car."

I'd like to offer $5,000 for a missing text—maybe you can help me find it. What part of the Bible teaches that when we face decisions that will affect the salvation of the lost, the church should vote on it? It isn't there. The only time a key decision was put to a majority vote in the Bible, they voted to return to Egypt. When the church in Jerusalem arrived at a make-or-break fork in the road, they didn't vote, they prayed.[90]

God leads by calling someone and placing on his heart an unquenchable passion. That person seeks God's will and commits himself to cooperating fully with the sovereign God. He then draws together a team of people whose hearts beat together for the cause. Together, the team wrestles with reality, trusts in God, then moves forward boldly to accomplish God's dream.

When it comes to designing the future, the role of the leadership team is to lead. Prayerfully, audaciously, strategically. For the singular purpose of building God's kingdom.

And the Church Manual Says...

I know what you're thinking: What about the *Church Manual?* Will it permit the leadership team to lead? Is it legal to structure in a way that isn't specified in the book?

Consider a little history. In the distant past, people rode to church either on or behind their horse. Their church was rural and small. Frequently, such a congregation was dominated by a single family who had built the church and insisted it was theirs. Or they controlled it for some other reason. The pastor or some other member might propose a great idea, but such an idea was dead-on-arrival if the dominant family disapproved. To protect against this nightmare scenario, the *Church Manual* prescribed a democratic process. Such a policy was invaluable then. It may or may not be in a larger church or one that chooses to be evangelistically aggressive.

The manual is not inspirationally equivalent to the Bible. The men and women who put it together never believed it had the non-negotiable authority of Scripture. It's rather a book of principles to protect us from going out in left field with our theology or from doing something that hinders the cause. Its intent is to help the work prosper. Whatever you can do to expand the impact of the local church honors that objective and harmonizes with the manual. It's like a Stop sign when you're on your way to the hospital to have a baby. If cars are coming, stop! If the road is clear, hurry on through and get to the hospital before your baby is delivered on the bucket seats.

Church leaders have amended the manual repeatedly to reflect ever-changing realities in the church and in society—and they will do so again. In the meantime, perhaps your church could maintain the spirit and the letter of the law by voting in a business meeting that issues specifically related to reaching the lost will, from now on, be entrusted to the leadership team.

An Effective Leadership Team
The ideal church leadership team has seven people, maybe even fewer in some situations. A team larger than seven has a hard time staying focused on the big picture.

Who should be on your team? Here's how to decide. Every leadership team member should:

(1) Daily submit his or her life to the will of God.

(2) Consistently prioritize his or her time to build friendships with the unchurched.

(3) Serve in a ministry.

(4) Love the pastor, and pray for him or her every day.

(5) Possess the spiritual gifts of leadership, discernment and faith.

Don't make the mistake of putting someone on the leadership team just because he or she has been around forever. Make sure that every member meets the qualifications above.

Another caution. It's a rare person who has more than 3-5 hours a week to give to ministry in the church. So if someone's time is limited and they are gifted to lead a ministry, don't consume their precious time on a decision-making board so they don't have time to lead in ministry.

Choose your leadership team prayerfully. Make them accountable to the congregation in some appropriate way. Then, for the sake of the gospel, let them lead.

Core Ministries

After the leadership team, the church's second structural level is your core ministries. Core means essential. Without these ministries, your church cannot be evangelistically effective. You may turn the lights on once a week and fellowship with the already-convinced, but to be a church of impact, you need these four or five core ministries (or a version thereof).

Worship

Sabbath worship is the hub of church life; it's the one time when all of the believers—and a number of unbelievers—gather to worship God. When church leaders understand the enormous potential for life-change for both members and guests in worship, they make a major investment of planning and time.

Outreach

A church without outreach is not really a church. Maybe a social club, but not a church. Faithfulness to the gospel commission demands that the church does everything it can to help lost people find Jesus. Picture the evangelism scale. By definition, outreach includes everything a church does (other than the worship experience) that connects with people left of the cross and moves them step-by-step toward salvation.

Discipleship

Once people come to Christ, its up to the church to help them grow spiritually with the goal that people embrace the character and priorities of Jesus. While outreach brings people to the cross, discipleship starts at that point and moves them a notch at a time on the evangelism scale toward spiritual maturity.

Administration

While the purpose of the church is clearly spiritual, the church has elements of a business. Finances, buildings, selection of leaders, membership records, and communication are all examples of things that must be administered well if the church is to grow.

Pre-adults

If a church is to grow, its leaders cannot give half-baked support to pre-adult ministry; they must do whatever it takes and pay any price to offer an outstanding ministry for children and young people. Consequently, some churches consider this a fifth core ministry; others place pre-adults under discipleship.

Machine or Living Organism?

With the core ministries chosen, it's time to consider the two basic ways of structuring an organization. The first is like a machine. A machine has a fixed list of parts. It's easy to maintain. Once it's up and running, all you have to do is squirt in a little oil, make a few adjustments, and listen to it hum. When a part wears out, you replace it with a different part and you're back in business. There's just one problem: machines don't grow. They're designed to accomplish a fixed task, but they remain pretty much the same size year after year after year.

Most churches are designed like a machine. In the Adventist church, the manual names a fixed list of parts. When a part quits or its term of service expires, you employ the nominating committee and you're back in business. The machine sputters to life again and produces a predictable product for another year. But it cannot grow.

The system of church structure outlined in the *Church Manual* is a blueprint for a small to medium-sized church. It assumes that every church is approximately the same size, is comprised of people with the same mix of spiritual gifts, and that every community has precisely the same needs. It served its purpose well in a previous era, and still does in some rural areas, but it all-too-often stifles creativity, pays little attention to spiritual gifts, and impedes numerical growth.

The second way to structure an organization is like a living organism. Organisms are the opposite of machines in several ways. First, they are high maintenance. Cats groom their fur.

Cows chew their cud and have to be milked. People take a bath, brush their teeth, comb their hair, feed their mouth—and the list goes on. Second, a living organism has considerable potential for growth.

A long time ago, my wife and I brought our daughter home from the hospital. She was so tiny it was hard to believe. Her head could lie on my hand and her toes didn't even touch my elbow. Today, Jana is in her twenties and a half-inch shorter than I am (in spite of her hope to someday be taller than Dad). She is a living organism. She started small, but was designed by the Creator to grow many times bigger. How? Through the division of cells with the DNA to grow and reproduce.

Is it possible to structure the church like a living organism, with virtually unlimited potential for growth? Absolutely. It's based on a simple principle called the fractal system. Compared to the nominating committee model, it is high maintenance, but the effect is powerful.

Draw a circle and bisect it vertically and horizontally. Plot one ministry in each of the quadrants. (If you consider *Pre-adult* to be a core ministry, divide the circle into five sections.) You are beginning to organize according to the fractal system.

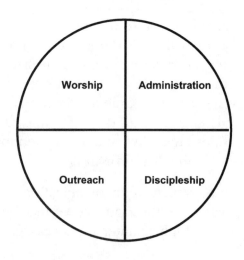

Next to each ministry, place the name of someone whom God has gifted with both leadership potential and a passion for that ministry. The pastor works closely with the four (or five) leaders and does everything he can to help them prosper. In harmony with Jethro's counsel to Moses, the pastor becomes a leader of ten.

Here's how: Most leaders in the church are married. Not all, but most. Imagine that Marla is your outreach leader. She does an excellent job with the ministry but her family is falling apart. How long will it be till the ministry is affected? The pastor does everything in his power to help Marla succeed professionally, but also feels concern for her as a whole person. He holds her accountable for a balanced personal and family life and provides support if and when it's needed.

Counting the four or five leaders under him and their spouses, adding himself and his own spouse, the pastor is indeed a leader of ten: Five in the professional arena; those five and their spouses in personal and spiritual matters.

Let's use Marla as an example. Once she agrees to be the Outreach leader, what is the first thing she does? She divides her cell (living organisms grow through cell division). Taking into consideration all of the opportunities and responsibilities of the Outreach ministry, Marla divides them into four. She draws her own circle and plots each of those in one of the quadrants.

For the sake of illustration, let's say her four divisions of the outreach ministry are:
   (a) Friendship Evangelism
   (b) Servant Evangelism
   (c) Bible Study Evangelism
   (d) Reaping Evangelism

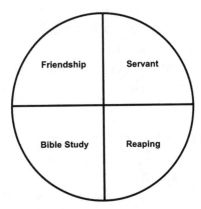

She now has four places where the right person could serve and thus contribute to the effectiveness of the ministry. She places her own name in each of the four quadrants while she begins to pray and search for people to serve in her ministry.

As soon as someone joins her team and one of the quadrants is filled, Marla is now on two fractal teams. She's a member of the pastor's team but she herself leads her own team. Every person, then, is a follower (part of the pastor's fractal), a leader (of her own fractal) and a recruiter. Eventually she fills each of her quadrants with a name and helps each quadrant divide its cell.

Move it down another level. Let's say Kenneth has agreed to lead Friendship Evangelism. What does he do first? He divides his cell. He considers all the opportunities and responsibilities of Friendship Evangelism, then divides them into four. He draws his own circle, plots his four ministry openings, and begins to pray and search for people to serve in his ministry. He now is a follower, a leader, and a recruiter.

Picture the same thing with Worship, Discipleship and Administration. The number of ministry openings is virtually unlimited. And like the cells of a living organism, the structure serves a church of 20 or 2,000 and allows for growth to any level.[91]

High maintenance? Yes. But only within one's own fractal; no leader has to be concerned with more than four or five positions. (As a living organism, your body is high maintenance, but you don't have to brush anyone's teeth but your own.) It's manageable. It's dynamic. And it releases people to serve according to their passion and their spiritual gifts while allowing for unlimited growth.

Free-market Groups

The third level of structure in your church—after the leadership team and your core ministries—is small groups. Grab your chisel and your hunk of granite because this next statement is supremely vital and positively non-negotiable. *Your church cannot grow bigger without growing smaller at the same time.* Brett Eastman, membership pastor at Saddleback Community Church, says it like this: "If you don't figure out how to get smaller as you're getting larger, growth will definitely peak."[92] The way to accomplish that is through small groups.

An effective small group system allows the advantages of a small church to coexist with the advantages of a large church. A small church specializes in the personal touch and intimacy. A large church offers a multitude of ministry options, a myriad of affinity groups and corporate worship that rivals Sabbath morning at camp meeting. A church that organizes properly captures the best of both worlds. So how do you grow bigger while growing smaller? By putting in place a small group system.

You've probably read about small groups. You may have experimented with them a time or two. You know the Biblical mandate. Acts 2 reports that the believers "broke bread from house to house."[93] Add to that Acts 20:20 and other passages and it's clear that small groups were foundational to church structure in the New Testament. Ellen White weighs in with an oft-quoted and convincing sentence, "The formation of small companies as a basis for Christian effort has been shown to me by one who cannot err."[94]

So small groups are God's idea and they're necessary to continued growth of the kingdom. But how on earth do you implement them in a way that actually works? How can you get the lion's share of the members to attend? What do you have to do to make the groups evangelistic? And, hardest of all, how do you keep the groups going week after month after year?

The answer is Free-market Groups. What are they? A means of organizing small groups that matches the inherent advantages of groups to the realities of Western culture.[95] They have three defining characteristics.

1. Free-market groups include everyone, whether left or right of the cross.

When an Adventist says she belongs to a small group, you know what she means. Everyone sits in a circle in someone's home or at the church and studies a Christian book, or maybe the Bible itself. This is perfect for those who (a) are far enough along on the evangelism scale to be interested in such a group, and (b) have the right personality.

Let me explain. Lazarus and his sisters lived in Bethany. When Jesus came to town, they were honored to have Him as part of the family—they knocked themselves out to make Him feel at home. The moment Jesus appeared, Mary dropped everything and sat at His feet. Simultaneously, Martha became a blur of human lightening in the kitchen, preparing her very best dishes for Jesus.

Mary was astounded that when Jesus came to town, Martha was so uninterested in Him that instead of hanging on His every word, she was out in the kitchen. Martha couldn't believe that when Jesus came to town, Mary was so lazy that she wouldn't help fix the meal.

Which sister loved Jesus more? I don't think you can say. Both of them loved Jesus but they demonstrated it according to how God wired them up, consistent with their individual personalities.

Some members love to sit at Jesus feet. Others show their love by serving. One isn't better; neither is right or wrong. It's just the way it is. When you offer only one type of small group—the "sit-in-a-circle," Bible study group—you meet the needs of those with a Mary personality but not Martha's.

No matter how hard you try—you can beg, plead, teach, pray, shame and bribe—you will not get Martha to sit in a circle and study the Bible for very long. The best she can muster is a month or two, or maybe the better part of a year. But she will always be fighting the way God made her. You'll be tempted to conclude that she doesn't love Jesus as much as someone who sticks it out forever. But you'd be wrong. You can't make Martha into Mary.

You need a second type of group for believers: a Ministry group. Its primary purpose is not to sit at Jesus' feet but to prepare His meals. Instead of sitting in a circle and praying, studying and encouraging, this group exists to accomplish something for Jesus. No doubt they will pray; they will sometimes share a Scripture and often encourage someone who is having a tough time. But their essential reason for getting together is to do something for the kingdom.

By designing groups to include both Mary and Martha, you've just doubled your attendance in small groups. You've potentially included everyone who is right of the cross on the evangelism scale.[96]

But you're not done yet. What about people who are still left of the cross and don't have an interest in either studying something spiritual or in serving? If your only small groups are for the already-convinced—if all they do is study Christian topics or pray—they'll never reach the lost. No problem. The free-market system includes two kinds of groups for those left of the cross. And as you would expect, those groups also correspond to the Mary and Martha personality types.

The first left-of-cross group is called a Needs group. The primary purpose is to connect with someone who doesn't know Christ and meet a need. So offer a class on finances and budgeting, or weight loss, or self-esteem, parenting, building a strong marriage, or grief recovery. Persons with a Mary personality (and a need) fit right in. The group's objective is to make friends, serve them, and help them move one notch closer to the cross.

The second left-of-cross group is a Recreation or Social group. Suppose your neighbor has no interest in the book of Daniel. He couldn't be dragged by the scruff of his neck to serve in a ministry or learn about parenting. But what if he likes target shooting or restoring old cars? What if she's into scrap booking or ceramics? Or golf or basketball? Start a group for her. The primary purpose is recreation, to connect with someone who isn't ready for something spiritual and by making friends, help them move one notch right.

Can you consider a biking group a legitimate small group? Certainly. As long as something overtly spiritual happens in the group each time you meet. It might be a short prayer before you go thanking God for good weather, healthy bodies and friends. It could be someone who shares a story while you're creating your scrap book. Maybe a Bible text when teaching on the topic of weight loss.

So now you have four types of groups, two for people right of the cross, and two for those left. With a proper balance between them, you have opportunities for people of both personality types to enjoy the benefits of a small group whether they're a +6 on the evangelism scale or they're way to the left of the cross.

Let's redraw the Evangelism Scale and plot our groups.

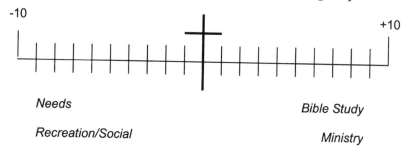

-10   +10

Needs   Bible Study

Recreation/Social   Ministry

The sky is the limit when it comes to the groups. Here's a sampling of some of the free-market groups in various churches:

- How to spend time with God and love it
- Watching World War II videos
- Computer basics
- Servant evangelism
- Building a hover craft
- Experiencing God
- How to share Jesus with your friends
- The life of Jesus
- Golf
- God Mob (for youth)
- Target shooting
- Marriage Matters
- Grief recovery
- Volleyball
- Biking

2. Free-market groups divide the calendar year into trimesters.

The second defining characteristic of free-market groups is they have a defined starting and ending time. In First World countries, it is counter-cultural to expect groups to continue to meet year after year until Jesus comes.

Football season doesn't last all year without a break. Baseball doesn't go on forever (it just seems like it). Sports fans know that when the Super Bowl is over, it's time to shift gears to basketball. When the NBA Finals are done, we'll check out baseball. Even nature teaches us the same. Trees and plants grow for a time, then stop, take a breath, and resume their growth the following season.

In the free-market system, the year is organized into trimesters, similar to those on a university campus. Winter trimester is 16 weeks (from January through April). Summer trimester is 12 weeks, followed by a Fall trimester of 16 weeks. In between, everyone has time off and gears up for the next trimester. If a group goes well and wants to continue, they're encouraged to do so. If a leader needs to take a break for whatever reason, it's OK. He or she can dive back into the fray when the following trimester rolls around.

3. Free-market groups maximize success and eliminate failure.

The third characteristic of free-market groups is the reason they are called "free-market." The free market is ruthless, but it also allows for virtually unlimited opportunity.

Let's suppose you open a restaurant that serves chicken and no one shows up. What do you do? Something else. No one cries over your failure but you. And you have no choice but to find something that fills a need.

Now imagine you establish a restaurant that serves chicken in the little town of Corbin, Kentucky. Customers love it, they tell their friends, and the place is packed. What do you do? Start another one. And yet another. You wouldn't think of turning people away so you franchise your success. You call it Kentucky Fried Chicken and before long you have a restaurant in every state and, eventually, all over the world.

It's the same in the church. Free-market groups give everyone a chance. You decide to start a dog-grooming group. In spite of your passion and your expertise, no one shows up. What do you do? Something else.

Suppose that your next attempt is a divorce recovery group. Thirty-seven people appear. What do you do? The best you can for that 12 or 16 week period. As the new semester gets close, you find someone to lead a second divorce recovery group while you lead one yourself.

The principle is simple: If something succeeds, do more of it. If it doesn't, don't worry about it, just do something else. It's the free-market way. The strongest and healthiest groups multiply while the weakest groups dissolve.

The church coordinates it all. Between each trimester, someone prints up a card or a booklet listing all of the groups. Group leaders and other members scatter the card around the neighborhood; they drop it off in apartment complexes, grocery stores and office buildings. Members give copies to their friends and work associates. Unchurched people are able to connect if and when they want with a group who participates in or studies something that interests them.

Organizing For Growth

Now put it all together. What you have is a structure in which everyone gets loved and everyone gets to serve. Energy is focused. Effort is maximized. Synergy happens as ministry opportunities abound.

First, empower your leadership team to oversee the direction of the church. Let them wrestle with God to discover His vision. Pray that they will make courageous decisions to move the kingdom ball down the field, to do whatever it takes to honor God.

Next, identify your core ministries and match the right leader to each one. Mentor that person so he or she becomes both a leader and a recruiter by dividing their cell and drawing others into service.

Last, grow smaller while you grow bigger through a free-market group system. Give everyone a chance to connect with others around an interest, a topic, a need or a cause. Pray that each one who attends, whether they are left or right of the cross, will move one notch closer to becoming a definitely devoted disciple of Jesus.

You've heard it somewhere before: Every church stops growing when the price gets too high. If your structure has hindered your growth, do the right thing. Bust through the stained-glass ceiling and build a structure that encourages progress.

---

84   Peter Drucker, *The Effective Executive*, p. 71.

85   1 Peter 2:5.

86   It's important to understand that the right structure won't cause growth, but the wrong structure, or no structure, will prevent the church from growing.

87   Thanks to Lonnie Gienger for this analogy.

88   Rick Warren, *The Purpose Driven Church*, p. 378.

89   His title is actually "Directional Leader;" in our lingo he would be called the pastor.

90   See Acts 6:1-7.

91   For an excellent explanation of the fractal system of church organization, read Wayne Cordeiro's *Doing Church As a Team* and watch his video series by the same title. Both resources are available at www.enewhope.org.

92   Quoted in Elmer Towns, *Into the Future*, p. 187.

93   Verse 46.

94   Ellen White, *Testimonies*, Vol. 7, p. 21.

95   For a thorough understanding of free-market groups and how to implement them, read *Dog Training, Fly Fishing and Sharing Christ*, by Ted Haggard.

96   The terms Mary and Martha, of course, are gender inclusive. Men have the same personality leanings.

HABIT

VISION

A *clear vision, along with the courage to follow through, dramatically increases your chances of coming to the end of your life, looking back with a deep, abiding satisfaction, and thinking, I did it. I succeeded. I finished well. My life counted.*

—Andy Stanley

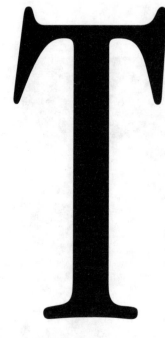

Two Eskimos are sitting on the ice, side by side, fishing poles in hand. The first has dropped his line through a tiny hole. He seems content to hope for a small fish or two. His buddy is different. His hole in the ice is enormous. It stretches all the way to the horizon—and it's shaped like a whale. The caption under the cartoon is one word: Vision.

How big is your fishing hole? How significant is your vision? "Where there is no vision," the good Book says, "your neighbors—and a lot of others–will perish."[97]

I was new in the conference as ministerial director. I asked a pastor to tell me his vision. His answer was as eerie as a séance. "I'm actually happy with the way things are right now," he began. "The conference is always pressuring me to baptize someone, but I basically ignore them." The smirk on his face reminded me of David Letterman.

"I know there are a lot of people who don't go to any church around here," he continued, "but I don't get too bothered about it. We have our sign out. We turn the lights on every week. If they want to come, they know what to do. Besides, my hands are full taking care of the people who do show up." I felt a baseball in my throat; I hunted for words that never came.

"We can teach ourselves to see things the way they are," says Max DePree. "Only with vision can we begin to see things the way they can be."

The defining question is this: What can be? What does God have in mind for your church? If Jesus were physically present at your next leadership meeting, what might He say? In what ways would He challenge you? Encourage you? Appeal to you?

God was no doubt present when Ellen White cast this vision: "The members of the church should give diligent attention to the word of God, that they may understand their duty and then labor with all their energies of the mind and heart to make their church one of the most prosperous in the land."[98]

Dream out loud for God. Is it possible for your church to become "one of the most prosperous in the land?" What would happen if you focused your vision and your prayers in that direction? What if you allocated resources to that end? What if you and your fellow church leaders were willing to pay the price and believed that God is still sovereign? What if you were persistent and undeterred?

Survival, Success, Significance

Every church ministers at one of three levels. The first is Survival. The vast majority of North American churches—somewhere north of 90 percent—function at the first level. They are in survival mode. Their priority is to preserve what they already have. They make decisions based on what will help them hang onto status quo. At all costs, they must survive. You can feel this on Sabbath morning, and especially at board meetings. They are dangerously inward-focused.

All churches begin in survival mode (babies always begin life at the survival stage), but God is dishonored by a church that remains there forever.

Most churches move beyond survival to the second level: **Success**. They pray, plan, work—and God shows up. The church wins souls. A new facility appears and maybe an elementary school. The majority of the members are proud of their church and say, "This is a successful church!" Even people driving by might think, *That looks like a successful church.*

Few leaders are aware, however, that success, when it comes to doing church, is a temporary condition. Either the church moves to the next level or before they know it, they have drifted back to survival. No church votes to go back. ("There's a motion on the table that we go back to being a church of survival. All in favor, say 'aye'.") They never post on the bulletin board: *Big news! We're going back to survival!* It just happens, because success is a temporary condition.

Here's how it happens. The risk and innovation that brought progress are almost always abandoned to preserve success. Momentum grinds to a halt because they are afraid to lose what they've achieved and before they know it, they've regressed. They turn inward and have a phlegmatic attitude toward the lost. Their commitment to save the lost in their community is verbal at best.

A handful of churches reach the third level of doing church: **Significance**. A church called to significance believes that God has called it to make a major and ongoing impact on its city.

What is significance? Several definitions are possible. The church aspires to become "one of the most prosperous in the land." Or, the church determines to become a leading Christian influence in its city. However you define it, the leaders resolve to pay whatever price they must so the church can continue to make an ever-larger kingdom impact in its community.

It is vital to note that significance is more of a journey than a destination. It would be foolish and arrogant for a church to wave a banner that says, "We did it! We're significant! We're satisfied!" Significance can only happen when leaders make an inflexible, non-negotiable, never-ending choice to pay whatever price they must so the church can continue to make an ever-larger kingdom impact in its community.

Is that possible? Sure. Look at it two ways. First, if your aim is to be a leading Christian influence in your city, that's not a short-term proposition, especially if you live in Miami or Toronto. It's definitely possible, but it won't happen without years of passionate prayer, consistent leadership and sacrifice. The smaller the city, of course, the more quickly your church can become a leading influence.

There is also another way to look at it. Your church could be a leading Christian influence in a specific geographic area right now, or at least in the not-too-distant future. Consider the size of your church at present. Take into account the passion of your leaders and the fervor of your members to be a church of significance. Once you have in place a culture of outreach, commitment, fun and prayer, you could be a leading Christian influence in some area of town today.

Plot your church on the map. Then draw a circle around the church that denotes where your church could be a leading Christian influence today or in the very near future. As your church grows and becomes more significant, increase the radius of your circle.[99]

Lessons from the Spies

Rewind to the book of Numbers. Moses sent twelve spies to the Promised Land on a mission of espionage. For forty days they analyzed the people, scrutinized the cities, and picked the crops. They came back with grapes as big as cantaloupes. Their press conference, however, was a disaster. Tragically, the men who took the mike first looked at things through human eyes instead of through God's eyes.

"It's a great place," they conceded. "The milk and honey are splendid. The fruit is colossal. It would be nice place to live. But don't get your hopes up. If you think the grapes are big, wait till you see the people; we're like grasshoppers compared to them. If we showed our face across the river, they'd stomp us into the ground. We'd be committing suicide to venture anywhere close."

The crowd wailed pathetically as hope morphed into panic—then further into rebellion.

Caleb and Joshua were men of faith. "Let us go up at once and take possession," they pleaded once the crowd settled down, "for we are well able to overcome it."[100]

You know what happened next. The people refused to believe. They were clear on what God intended, but they thought He was too weak to pull it off. As a result, they died in the desert.

Here's a fact: There are twelve spies inside each one of us. Ten are persuaded that what God has told us to do cannot be done; the giants are too portentous. The other two spies see the same realities but through different eyes. "If the Lord delights in us," they insist, "then He will bring us to this land."[101] Here's the bottom line—and it's really cool: We get to choose whether we will listen to the ten spies inside of us or to the two.

Factoring in God

The critics never factor in God. Think about it and I know you'll agree. Those who criticize when God says "Go for it!" fail to see with anointed eyes. They insist on the blinding perspective of those who live with spiritual eyes sealed shut. They pretend to have vision, but their spiritual white-tipped canes give them away.

Our church was looking for land. We were a new church—only 18 months old—but we wanted to snag a piece of land on which we could eventually erect a church facility. It seemed hopeless. We were mostly young families with small kids and smaller paychecks. Land in our area of town was $300,000 an acre and up.

Every Thursday afternoon I drove the streets, writing down the location of one plot of land after the other. I found out who owned it, made contact, and prayed for a miracle. Doors slammed in my face with sobering predictability.

One Sabbath afternoon we followed a picnic in the park with a church business meeting. One of the deacons stood to his feet. "Ron, everyone here knows that we will never be able to afford land. Every time we get together you try to pump us up and convince us that we will. You're not doing us any favor. The sooner we all admit it, the better off we'll all be. I suggest you lay off and stop talking about buying land."

His icy words slapped my face like the tail of a fish.

Suppose you're the pastor. What would you say next?

I started with a smile. It was fake, but it was the best I could muster. "Mark, let me thank you for pointing out the truth," I responded. "You're right on when you say that what we're trying to do is impossible—humanly speaking. So here's an assignment.

"I'd like you to write out what you just said—about never getting land because it's way beyond us. Put it on a sheet of paper. We'll buy a frame and make your note look really nice. Then when we move into our new church someday, we'll hang it on the wall in the lobby to remind ourselves that what happened was impossible without God."

The crowd was silent, especially Mark. All I could hear was my heart pounding and the Spirit saying, "According to your faith, let it be done unto you."[102] It was only a few months later that God smiled on us with a series of miracles that rival anything found in the book of Acts. We were able to purchase land worth more than a million dollars for a measly $35,000. Indeed, the critics never factor in God.

"We live by faith," Paul reported, "not by sight." In the church, it's so much easier to live by sight. If the path ahead is clear, we'll move in that direction. If it isn't, we're timid, anxious, even terrified.

We know the Bible stories. We teach them to our kids and discuss them in our Sabbath School classes. We say *Amen* when the pastor preaches on the story of the lion's den or David and Goliath. With our words, we declare that we believe the stories are true. Yet few of us are bold enough to ask God to intervene in ways that will dramatically honor Him and build up His kingdom.

Jesus couldn't do miracles in His hometown because of their inexcusable lack of faith. Our town is all too often His hometown; we might just as well live in Nazareth. He wants to bless us, but we limit His intervention with our disbelief.

If You Were God…

I was meeting with a group of wild-eyed church planters who love what they do and are chomping at the bit to make a bigger difference. We were discussing what it would take to grow each congregation into a church of significance. Out of the blue, one of the planters had a Nazareth moment—he referred to something as impossible. His statement assumed that we serve a god of scarcity rather than a God of abundance.

"Let's have some fun," I suggested. "Think about your church plant. Consider your leaders, your recent baptisms, the guests who come from time to time to check you out. Take into account the money you have in the bank, the building where you meet, all your equipment. You know, everything that has to do with your plant. Got it?

"Now assume you're convinced that God wants your church to become a church of significance. Tell me what you need. What's holding you back? Tell me what should go in this blank and I'll write it on the flip chart: *If we just had _____, we could take a major step in our journey toward significance.*"

The first church planter to speak said, "a million dollars." His answer raised a few eyebrows. "Explain why you need a million dollars," I insisted.

"We have two hundred people attending every Sabbath. We can't find a decent place to meet. We need to grab a piece of land and build on it. I've been driving around town and found the perfect lot—great location, ideal size—and we need a million dollars to buy it. I know that would fire people up and it wouldn't be long until we'd have a fantastic place to meet and we'd fill it up!"

I wrote "One Million Dollars" on the flip chart.

The next planter raised his hand. "We need 15 million dollars."

I rolled my eyes and grinned. "OK, convince me." I could hardly wait to hear this one!

"My conference president announced at our last pastors' meeting that we need to plant 30 new churches as quickly as possible. I've done the math. If we had 15 million dollars, we could hire a church planter for every one of them, give them some funding to get started, add staff to the ones that grow, and help them make a payment on some land."

It sounded good to me, so I wrote "15 Million Dollars" on the flip chart.

The rest of the responses were a bit more modest. But they all represented things that were impossible unless God intervened. We filled up two flip chart pages with what the planters believed they needed to move toward significance.

"Now here's the deal," I chose my words deliberately. "I have in my hand a red marker. We're going to go through this list as a group, line by line. As we do, let's identify which of these requests are so vast and so impossible that not even God could make them happen. I'll draw a big, red circle around those, and that way we'll know better than to ask God for them because, clearly, they're beyond even God. OK? Let's go!"

At first it was silent. The mental wheels were spinning. But it wasn't long until their faces changed from contemplation to resolve. And one-by-one, they insisted that none of our needs are beyond the reach of God. We ended our session in earnest prayer that God would clarify to each of us what we really need, then grant us the faith to lay hold of His divine blessing so that our churches can indeed impact their communities with unstoppable power.

"The first-century church," Erwin McManus writes, "was founded on the adventurous journeys of men like Paul and Barnabas. It was never intended to be a place of safety from the rapidly changing world. The church should be the greatest revolution ever initiated on this planet. She moves from generation to generation through the dreamers and visionaries who believe that nothing is impossible with God. And like prophets, they call God's people to live their lives as if God is truly God."[103]

Ask yourself this question: If you were God, who would you bless? The church leader who resolves that the church cannot move forward until the path ahead is clear? The person who knows why his or her church has stopped reaching the lost but would rather be comfortable than to pay the price? Or would you bless the one whose heart burns within him or her to honor God by acting with dangerous faith for the rapid advance of the kingdom?

When the disciples concluded that the great multitude could not be fed, Jesus asked a simple question: "How many loaves do you have?"[104] Jesus was in their midst physically, they had seen miracle after miracle with their own eyes, and yet the disciples couldn't even imagine that He would do something supernatural in *this* situation. Followers of Jesus today know that five loaves and two fish are enough when they devote what they have to God and their deepest desire is to obey Christ's command.

Three Defining Questions

Every church says they want to win people to Christ. Are they just pretending or do they really mean it? Lock the doors and disable the cell phones at your next leadership meeting. Your agenda consists of three questions. Don't hold back. Be brutally honest. However long it takes—seize the whole weekend if you need to—come to agreement. Because the way you answer these questions, will determine whether your church remains mired in mediocrity or moves forward toward significance.

First, how big is the pastor's vision? Is he satisfied with the way things are or is he a leader who passionately seeks God's heart for the church?

Second, how significant do the members want the church to be? Talk is cheap. Actions speak louder than words. All too many church leaders confess with their tongue that they want the church to grow, but their actions reveal that they like the church pretty much like it is.

Third, is everyone willing to pay the price? The pastor cannot do it without the members; at the very least, the majority of the movers and the shakers need to be on board. If the pastor is willing but the members are not, he needs to shake the dust off his feet—with a smile on his face—and move on to another church.

Conversely, the members cannot do it without the pastor. If the members long to move toward significance but the pastor doesn't care, the members need to rent a U-Haul and help the pastor pack. If everyone is willing, hope breaks through like grass through concrete.

First the bad news: (a) Your price will be high; (b) Whatever your price is, it will not be a quick fix. But here is the good news: (a) God's resources are higher than your price; (b) If you prepare the horse, God will see to it that you win the battle. (See Proverbs 21:31.)

Vision sees what God sees—and the result is astonishing. Sort of like things that happened in the Bible. And since every church stops growing when the price is too high, why not seek God for vision and continue seeking until you find it?

THE 7 HABITS OF HIGHLY INEFFECTIVE CHURCHES

97 Paraphrase of Proverbs 29:18.

98 *Review & Herald,* September 6, 1911. The same author also says, "The apostle Paul, in his ministry among the churches, was untiring in his efforts to inspire in the hearts of the new converts a desire to do large things for the cause of God." *Counsels on Stewardship,* p. 171.

99 For a discussion of how a church can achieve significance, see my article "Building a Home Depot" at www.plantthefuture.org.

100 Numbers 13:30.

101 Numbers 14:8.

102 Matthew 9:29.

103 Erwin Raphael McManus, *An Unstoppable Force,* p. 140.

104 Mark 6:38; Mark 8:5.

THE 7 HABITS OF HIGHLY INEFFECTIVE CHURCHES

NOW WHAT?

A man should assault life with such energy that in dying, he would go out to meet the echo of his own shout.

—Sean O'Casey

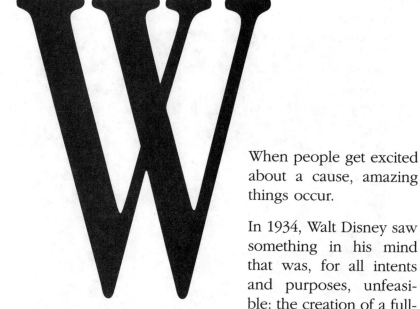

When people get excited about a cause, amazing things occur.

In 1934, Walt Disney saw something in his mind that was, for all intents and purposes, unfeasible: the creation of a full-length animated feature film. Defying all logic, he insisted that his employees create an eighty-three minute movie under the title *Snow White and the Seven Dwarfs*.

Try to put it into perspective. Seventy years ago, animation was extremely labor intensive; each frame of the picture had to be created literally by hand. Since xerography and computers were yet to be invented, a sequence as simple as a cow jumping over the moon required thousands of individual drawings. His associates and friends swore that to think that such a task could ever be completed was full-blown insanity.

Disney plugged his ears to their skepticism. As a starting point, he hired 300 commercial artists, potential artists, and architects from all over the world. Once employed, he gathered them together in an empty soundstage under a naked light bulb, and he acted out the entire story. Sitting on folding chairs, the men saw and heard Walt Disney personally act out every detail: Snow White's first encounter with the Seven Dwarfs, the individual foibles of the seven little men, the transformation of the Wicked Queen into the Wicked Witch, the brandishing of the poison apple, even the final kiss that brings the comatose heroine back to life.

His performance was no party stunt. The hours-long enactment was the living script the animators turned to again and again as they struggled to complete the film. In addition to the painstaking work of the artists, hundreds of non-animators from musicians to special effects technicians worked almost around the clock for three and a half years.

The finished product contained 250,000 individual drawings (a baby rabbit, a character of utmost triviality, required 43 separate sketches) and cost a then mind-boggling sum of $1.5 million. When the movie debuted on December 21, 1937, it blew away every box-office record, bringing in $8 million in its first year. The visionary had become a hero.[105]

If talented and dedicated people can be recruited to make a movie about a harassed princess and seven simulated dwarfs, could it be that the cause to which God has called us would infect Christ-followers today with irrational and irrevocable vision?

One of my friends is a church planter. He's also as crazy as Walt Disney, maybe crazier. (One definition for crazy in the dictionary is intensely enthusiastic about or preoccupied with something. Using that definition, he's undeniably crazy.)

Shane sent me an e-mail that proves he doesn't think like most people do. That, of course, comes from his vision which grows out of his prayer life and affects everything he does. It places him in a group that, numerically, is small, but one that God uses to make a big difference. Here's what he said, word for word. The italics and bold letters are his.

We have recently agreed to take seriously our commission from God to reach everyone in our area (about

40,000+ people within just a few square miles of us, tens of thousands more within a few miles after that) with Jesus and the Three Angels Message. We are content with whomever God chooses to send our way. But we also firmly believe that it would bring glory to God to have an SDA church that *intentionally chooses and strategically plans to never stop growing until all are reached in a given area.*

Now I don't know of many churches that officially vote to stop reaching people for Jesus. Yet one look at most Adventist churches' histories will quickly tell us that nearly all of them do stop reaching out and stop growing. One very curious fact about this is that this stoppage generally occurs at between 50 and 250 in attendance—and this is so regardless of whether a church is in a town of 600 or 600,000!

Think of the unreached masses of people! We don't believe this is God's will for Lake Stevens. So we are formulating specific plans to break through whatever growth barriers the devil may place in our path. *Every soul matters* to God, and there are 40,000+ of them here that God wants to be prepared for the final events in earth's history.

His e-mail ended with this sentence in bold: **"Please pray that God will give us wisdom as we make plans to reach literally all of our area for Jesus."**[106]

Thom Rainer spoke for every faith-filled follower of Christ when he announced, "I have entered the land of miracles, and I do not wish to return."[107] David was crazy to confront Goliath. Elisha was crazy to expect an iron axe head to float. A handful of disciples heard Jesus instruct them to "make disciples of all the nations" and were crazy enough that they decided to obey and see what would happen. And you are crazy if you think that God will use your church to make a dramatic difference in the population of heaven.

But—and don't miss this—you're even crazier if you claim to follow Jesus and you don't have faith in His Word. You're *foolish, impractical or senseless* (another dictionary definition for *crazy*) if you read the stories of God's spectacular intervention and don't believe He is able or willing today. He is honored when you ask Him for large favors that you might bring glory to His name.[108]

The best speech at the 1996 Democratic National Convention was not given by Bill Clinton (who was running for re-election) or Al Gore (his vice president). It was given, instead, by a former actor who sat in a wheelchair—Christopher Reeve. Here, in part, is what he said.

> On the wall of my room when I was in rehab was a picture of the space shuttle blasting off, autographed by every astronaut now at NASA. On top of the picture it says, 'We found that nothing is impossible.'
>
> That should be our motto. Not a Democratic motto, not a Republican motto, but an American motto. Because this is not something one party can do alone. It's something we as a nation must do together.
>
> So many of our dreams at first seem impossible. Then they seem improbable. And then, when we summon the will, they soon become inevitable.

It is inevitable that this work will be finished. It is inevitable that God will fulfill His promise. It is inevitable that God will find men and women of extraordinary boldness and faith. And when He does, He will bless them and use them without measure.[109] The day will come when the Gospel Commission will be completed in your town. At some not-too-distant point, this world will end and Jesus will return.

God raised up your church for a reason. Your church is the hope for your community. Jesus deserves your church to be the way He envisioned when He died on the cross. So bring your leaders together, agree on what you need to do, then focus on one habit at a time. Whatever it takes, move forward boldly with the vigor of fissioning uranium.

As you have turned the pages of this book, you have learned why churches stop growing. You have likely put your finger on one more reasons that apply to your church. What happens next? You decide. You can set it all aside and wish things would change. Or you can fall to your knees and plead with God for wisdom and for the courage to make a difference. It all depends on your commitment to Christ, your love for the lost, and on your vision.

There are no shortcuts to anywhere worth going. Don't look for shortcuts. Since every church stops growing when the price gets too high, be willing to pay the price. And someday God—along with a lot of redeemed souls—will break into the biggest smile you've ever seen, throw His arms around you, and say "thanks!"

Must-read Books

1. An Unstoppable Force (Erwin McManus)
2. Conspiracy of Kindness (Steve Sjogren)
3. Courageous Leadership (Bill Hybels)
4. Dog Training, Fly Fishing, and Sharing Christ (Ted Haggard)
5. Good to Great (Jim Collins)
6. Leading Beyond the Walls (Adam Hamilton)
7. One Size Doesn't Fit All (Gary McIntosh)
8. Plant the Future (Ron Gladden)

9. Seizing Your Divine Moment (Erwin McManus)
10. Surprising Insights from the Unchurched (Thom Rainer)
11. The 21 Irrefutable Laws of Leadership (John Maxwell)
12. The Purpose Driven Church (Rick Warren)
13. The Very Large Church (Lyle Schaller)
14. Visioneering (Andy Stanley)

105   The facts of the movie's creation were taken from Warren Bennis and Patricia Ward
      Biederman, *Organizing Genius*, p. 36-49.

106   Received from Shane Anderson.

107   Thom Rainer, *Surprising Insights from the Unchurched*, p. 234.

108   See Ellen White, *The Desire of Ages*, p. 668.

109   See Ellen White, *Christian Service*, p. 254.

Published by
The Washington Post
1150 15th Street, N.W.
Washington, D.C. 20071

First Edition

© 1996 by The Washington Post

No part of this book may be reproduced or transmitted in any
form or by any means, electronic or mechanical, including
photocopying, recording, or by any information storage and
retrieval system, without written permission from the publisher.

The text of this book is composed in Times New Roman, with
the display in Gill Sans.

Manufactured in the United States by Chroma Graphics, Largo, MD
in association with Alan Abrams

ISBN: [0-9625971-3-9]

Publisher and Editor: Noel Epstein
Graphic Design: Robert Barkin, Barkin & Davis
Cover Illustration: Susan Davis, Barkin & Davis
Map on Page 226 by Dave Cook, The Washington Post